JUST DO SOMETHING

A LIBERATING APPROACH TO FINDING GOD'S WILL

KEVIN DEYOUNG

MOODY PUBLISHERS
CHICAGO

Unless otherwise indicated, all Scripture quotations are from *The Holy Bible, English Standard Version*. Copyright © 2000, 2001 by Crossway Bibles, a division of Good News Publishers. Used by permission. All rights reserved.

Scripture quotations marked NIV are taken from the *Holy Bible, New International Version*®. NIV®. Copyright © 1973, 1978, 1984 by International Bible Society. Used by permission of Zondervan. All rights reserved.

Published in association with the literary agency of Wolgemuth & Associates, Inc.

Editor: Jim Vincent
Interior Design: Ragont Design
Cover Design: Gearbox
Cover Image: Solus Photography/Beowulf Sheehan
Author Photo: © LCH Photography

Library of Congress Cataloging-in-Publication Data
DeYoung, Kevin.
  Just do something : a liberating approach to finding God's will /
  Kevin DeYoung.
     p. cm.
  Includes bibliographical references.
  ISBN 978-0-8024-5838-4
  1. Young adults—Religious life. 2. God (Christianity)—Will.
  3. Discernment (Christian theology) 4. Christian life—Reformed
  authors. I. Title.
  BV4529.2.D4 2009
  248.4—dc22
                                                        2008049382

We hope you enjoy this book from Moody Publishers. Our goal is to provide high-quality, thought-provoking books and products that connect truth to your real needs and challenges. For more information on other books and products written and produced from a biblical perspective, go to www.moodypublishers.com or write to:

Moody Publishers
820 N. LaSalle Boulevard
Chicago, IL 60610

9 10

Printed in the United States of America

To my hard-working, God-fearing,
wonderfully Dutch grandfathers,

Peter DeYoung and
Menser Vanden Heuvel

CONTENTS

FOREWORD

It is God's will for you to read this book. Yes, I'm talking to you. What are the odds that you would "just happen" to pick up this book and flip open to this page and start reading? Obviously it's a sign. Of all the millions of books in the world, you found this one. Wow. I have chills. Do not pass up this divinely orchestrated moment. If you miss this moment there's a good chance you will completely miss God's will for the rest of your life and spend your days in misery and regret.

Now that I've scared you, let me acknowledge that everything in the previous paragraph is total baloney. It's bunk. Not true at all. Actually, I don't know if it's God's will for you to read this book. But I do think that reading it could be a really good idea.

If you're prone to think of God's will in the way I so threateningly described it, this book will help set you straight. Kevin DeYoung is a skilled pastor, theologically astute, and a clear communicator. He gives you serious content but makes it easy to absorb and understand.

In *Just Do Something* Kevin will show what trips us up from moving forward in making decisions. He'll talk about how God speaks to us and what it means to be guided by wisdom. In a gentle and loving way he will challenge you.

There's a good chance that you've picked up some faulty ways of thinking about this issue. I love the no-nonsense way Kevin pulls us back to truth: "God is not a magic 8-ball we shake up and peer into whenever we have a decision to make. He is a good God who gives us brains, shows us the way of obedience, and invites us to take risks for him."

I'm a pastor. And the highest praise I can give this book is that this is my new go-to book on decision making and "finding God's will." If you were in my church and you came to me and said, "I have a big decision to make (marriage, job, house, etc), and I need to know what God wants me to do." I would put this book in your hands.

It's liberating and encouraging and even where it smacks you upside the head (which it does once in a while) you'll be better for the smack. You'll think more clearly and more biblically.

So read this book. You'll be wiser because of it.

Joshua Harris

Senior pastor of Covenant Life Church and author of *Stop Dating the Church!*

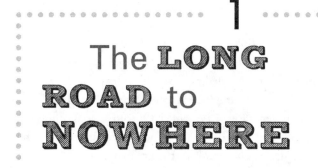

1

The **LONG ROAD** to **NOWHERE**

I grew up playing with Tinkertoys. Like most Americans over the past one hundred years, our family had the classic long tube full of sticks, wooden wheels, and colored connectors. Hitting the market in 1913, Tinkertoy (now owned by Hasbro) has sold about 2.5 million construction sets per year for almost a hundred years. The impetus for Tinkertoy construction sets—which initially sold for sixty cents and were called by the less-than-catchy name "Thousand Wonder Builders" —came from Charles Pajeau and Robert Petit, who dreamed up the toy as they watched children tinkering around with pencils, sticks, and empty spools of thread.

With almost a century gone by, there's still nothing fancy about Tinkertoy sets, especially in a digital age where children seldom go anywhere without microchips of entertainment close at hand. Kids still like Tinkertoys because kids like to tinker.

And apparently, so do adults.

In the book *After the Baby Boomers: How Twenty- and Thirty-Somethings are Shaping the Future of American Religion*, Robert Wuthnow describes twenty-one to forty-five-year-olds as tinkerers.[1] Our grandparents built. Our parents boomed. And my generation? We tinker. Of course, as Wuthnow points out, tinkering is not all bad. Those who tinker know how to improvise, specialize, pull things apart, and pull people together from a thousand different places. But tinkering also means indecision, contradiction, and instability. We are seeing a generation of young people grow up (sort of) who tinker with doctrines, tinker with churches, tinker with girlfriends and boyfriends, tinker with college majors, tinker living in and out of their parents' basement, and tinker with spiritual practices no matter how irreconcilable or divergent.

We're not consistent. We're not stable. We don't stick with anything. We aren't sure we are making the right decisions. Most of the time, we can't even make decisions. And we don't follow through. All of this means that as Christian young people we are less fruitful and less faithful than we ought to be.

Granted, youth tends to come with a significant amount of youthfulness. And with youthfulness comes indecision and instability. Young adults who tinker are not confined to any one generation. Baby boomers, and probably even builders (the generation that grew up during the Great Depression and fought in World War II), tinkered around with God and life when they were young adults. The difference, however, with my generation is that young adulthood keeps getting longer and longer. It used to be that thirty seemed old and far removed from youth, but now it is not uncommon to hear of folks "coming of age" at forty.

Consider this one statistic: In 1960, 77 percent of women and 65 percent of men completed all the major transitions into adulthood by age thirty. These transitions include leaving home, finishing school, becoming financially independent, getting married, and having a child. By 2000, only 46 percent of woman completed these transitions by age thirty, and only 31 percent of men.[2] It's stunning for me to think that less than a third of men my age are done with school, out of the house, married with kids, and have a job that pays the bills. "Adultolescence" is the new normal.

Now, I know there are lots of good reasons why someone may still be in school past thirty. After all, multiple college degrees take time. And I realize there are legitimate reasons why a thirty-year-old might have to live with his parents (e.g., illness, unexpected unemployment, or divorce). Concerning marriage, maybe you have the gift of celibacy. And as for a family, maybe you've been trying to have kids but can't. There are lots of reasons for delayed adulthood. I understand that. Just because you've been on the planet for one-fourth to one-third of your life and still haven't completed "the transition" to adulthood doesn't mean you're automatically a moocher, a lazy bum, or a self-indulgent vagabond.

But it could mean that. It is possible that your "unparalleled freedom to roam, experiment, learn (or not), move on, and try again" has not made you wiser, cultured, or more mature.[3] Perhaps your free spirit needs less freedom and more faithfulness. Maybe your emerging adulthood should . . . I don't know, emerge.

But let me be clear: This is not a book *just* for young people. I'm not going to attempt a generational analysis of my fellow thirtysomethings. I'm not issuing a new manifesto for baby busters and mosaics. This book is much simpler than all that. This is a book about God's will—God's will for confused teenagers, burned-out parents, retired grandparents, and, yes, tinkering millennials . . . or whatever we're called.

I bring up this whole business of adultolescence because it is related to the spiritual issue of God's will. You'll find in this book some of the typical will-of-God fare—how to make wise decisions, how to choose a job, whom to marry, etc. But answering these questions is not really the aim of this book. My goal is not as much to tell you how to hear God's voice in making decisions as it is to help you hear God telling you to get off the long road to nowhere and finally make a decision, get a job, and, perhaps, get married.

The hesitancy so many of us (especially the young) feel in making decisions and settling down in life and therefore diligently searching for the will of God has at least two sources. First, the new generations enjoy—or at least think they enjoy—"unparalleled freedom." Nothing is settled after high school or even college anymore. Life is wide open and filled with endless possibilities, but with this sense of opportunity comes confusion, anxiety, and indecision. *With everything I could do and everywhere I could go, how can I know what's what?* Enter a passion to discern "God's will for my life." That's a key reason there is always a market for books about the will of God.

Second, our search for the will of God has become an accomplice in the postponement of growing up, a convenient out for the young (or old) Christian floating through life without direction or purpose. Too many of us have passed off our instability, inconsistency, and endless self-exploration as "looking for God's will," as if not making up our minds and meandering through life were marks of spiritual sensitivity.

As a result, we are full of passivity and empty on follow-through. We're tinkering around with everyone and everything. Instead, when it comes to our future, we should take some responsibility, make a decision, and just do something.

2
THE WILL of GOD in CHRISTIANESE

If God has a wonderful plan for my life, as the evangelistic tract tells us, then why doesn't He tell me what it is?

After all, our lives down here are a confusing mess of fits and starts, dead ends and open doors, possibilities and competing ideals. There are so many decisions to make and none of the answers seem clear. What should I do this summer? What should my major be? What kind of career do I want? Do I want a career? Should I get married? Whom should I marry? Do I want kids? How many kids? Should I play sports or sing in the choir? Where should I go to college? Should I even go to college? Should I go to grad school? What job should I take? Should I stay in my current job? Should I be a missionary? Should I be a pastor? Should I volunteer here or there? Should I leave home and test the waters elsewhere? Is now the time to buy a house?

For some there are serious money, relationship, and even retirement questions. How should I spend my money? Where should I give my money? Where should I go to church? How should I serve my church? What should I be doing with the rest of my life, and where and with whom should I be doing it? When should I retire? What should I do in retirement?

With so many questions to face in the next years—or sometimes in the next several weeks—it's no surprise so many of us are desperate to know the will of God for our lives. Which brings me back to a rephrasing of the question that began this chapter: If God has a wonderful plan for my life, how can I discover what it is?

A lot of books have been written trying to answer this basic question, and my answer may not be what you expect from a will-of-God book. My answer is not original to me, but it is quite simple and, I hope, quite biblical. I'd like us to consider that maybe we have difficulty discovering God's wonderful plan for our lives because, if the truth be told, He doesn't really intend to tell us what it is. And maybe we're wrong to expect Him to.

ARE YOU CONFUSED YET?

"The will of God" is one of the most confusing phrases in the Christian vocabulary. Sometimes we speak of all things happening according to God's will. Other times we talk about being obedient and doing the will of God. And still other times we talk about finding the will of God. The confusion is due to our using the phrase "the will of God" in at least three different ways, typified in the previous three sentences. Two of these ways are clearly demonstrated in Scripture; the third is a little more complicated. So we'll start with the first two.

GOD ALWAYS GETS HIS WAY

If we examine the Bible, we see that God's will has two sides to it. On the first side is God's *will of decree.* This refers to what God has ordained. Everything that comes to pass is according to God's sovereign decree. And all that He decrees will ultimately come to pass. God's will of decree cannot be thwarted. It is immutable and fixed. God is sovereign over all things—nature and nations, animals and angels, spirits and Satan, wonderful people and wicked people, even disease and death. To steal a line from Augustine, "The will of God is the necessity of all things." In other words, what God wills, will happen, and what happens is according to God's will. That's what I mean by God's will of decree.

God's will of decree is taught in numerous passages of Scripture:

> *Ephesians 1:11:* "In him we have obtained an inheritance, having been predestined according to the purpose of him who works all things according to the counsel of his will."

God works out everything—the big picture, the little details, and everything in between—according to His own good and sovereign purposes.

Matthew 10:29–30: "Are not two sparrows sold for a penny?
    And not one of them will fall to the ground apart from your
    Father. But even the hairs of your head are all numbered."

God micromanages our lives. He doesn't just plan out a
few of the big ticket items. Praise the Lord, He knows the
smallest sparrow and the grayest hair. And neither falls to the
ground unless our heavenly Father wills it.

Acts 4:27–28: "For truly in this city there were gathered to-
    gether against your holy servant Jesus, whom you
    anointed, both Herod and Pontius Pilate, along with the
    Gentiles and the peoples of Israel, to do whatever your
    hand and your plan had predestined to take place."

Every human lamentation and woe must look to the cross.
For there we see the problem of evil "answered"—not in some
theoretical sense—but by pointing us to an all-powerful God
who works all things for good. Shocking as it sounds, the most
heinous act of evil and injustice ever perpetrated on the
earth—the murder of the Son of God—took place according
to God's gracious and predetermined will.

Psalm 139:16: "Your eyes saw my unformed substance; in your
    book were written, every one of them, the days that were
    formed for me, when as yet there were none of them."

Our lives unfold, open and close, according to God's providence. As the crafters of the Heidelberg Catechism put it so
eloquently back in the sixteenth century, "Providence is the

almighty and ever present power of God by which he upholds, as with his hand, heaven and earth and all creatures, and so rules them that leaf and blade, rain and drought, fruitful and lean years, food and drink, health and sickness, prosperity and poverty–all things, in fact, come to us not by chance, but from his fatherly hand."[1]

> *Isaiah 46:9–10:* "I am God, and there is no other; I am God and there is none like me, declaring the end from the beginning and from ancient times things not yet done, saying, 'My counsel shall stand, and I will accomplish all my purpose.'"

God knows all things and sovereignly superintends all things. God's will of decree is absolute. It is from before the creation of the world. It is the ultimate determination over all things, and it cannot be overturned.

GOD POINTS OUT THE WAY

The other side of the coin is God's *will of desire.* This refers to what God has commanded—what He desires from His creatures. If the will of decree is how things are, the will of desire is how things ought to be. I realize that I am not dealing with the massive question of how God can decree all that comes to pass while also holding us responsible for our actions. That's the old divine sovereignty and human responsibility question. The Bible clearly affirms both. For example, God sent Babylon to punish Judah, but God also punished Babylon for acting wickedly against God's people (Jeremiah 25). Likewise, God planned the death of His Son and yet those who killed the Christ were called lawless men (Acts 2:23). I believe there are theological categories that can help us reconcile divine sovereignty and human responsibility, but diving into these ideas would take us far beyond the scope of this short book. I am simply noting that God is sovereign, but He is not the author of sin. We are under His sovereignty, but we are not free from responsibility for our actions.

Both sides of God's will are in Scripture. God's will of decree —what He has predetermined from eternity past—cannot be thwarted. God's will of desire—the way He wants us to live— can be disregarded.

Let me highlight a few passages that speak of God's will as His will of desire:

> *1 John 2:15–17:* "Do not love the world or the things in the world. If anyone loves the world, the love of the Father is not in him. For all that is in the world—the desires of the flesh and the desires of the eyes and pride in possessions—is not from the Father but is from the world. And the world is passing away along with its desires, but whoever does the will of God abides forever."

The will of God in this passage does not refer to the way God ordains things, but to the way God commands us to live. Walking in the will of God for the apostle John is the opposite of worldliness. Doing the will of God means we say no to the desires of the flesh, the desires of the eyes, and our pride in possessions.

Hebrews 13:20–21: "Now may the God of peace who brought again from the dead our Lord Jesus, the great shepherd of the sheep, by the blood of the eternal covenant, equip you with everything good that you may do his will, working in us that which is pleasing in his sight, through Jesus Christ, to whom be glory forever and ever. Amen."

The will of God, as His will of desire, means that we do what is pleasing in His sight.

Matthew 7:21: "Not everyone who says to me, 'Lord, Lord,' will enter the kingdom of heaven, but the one who does the will of my Father who is in heaven."

Again, we see the will of God is shorthand for obedience to God's commands and walking in His ways—this time from the lips of Christ Himself.

Deuteronomy 29:29: "The secret things belong to the Lord our God, but the things that are revealed belong to us and to our children forever, that we may do all the words of this law."

This is the closest we come to finding the will of decree and will of desire side by side in the same verse. God has secret things known only to Him (His inscrutable purposes and sovereign will), but He also has revealed things that we are meant to know and obey (His commands and His Word).

DOES GOD HAVE A
SPECIFIC PLAN FOR YOUR LIFE?

There's a third way in which we sometimes speak of God's will. Most of the time what we really are looking for is God's *will of direction.*

We hear it in those questions we asked at the beginning of this chapter: What does God want me to do with my life? What job should I take? Where should I live? Those are the questions we ask when we seek God's will of direction. We want to know His individual, specific plan for the who, what, where, when, and how of our lives. We want to know His direction.

> Stop thinking of God's will like a corn maze, or a tightrope, or a bull's-eye.

So here's the real heart of the matter: Does God have a secret will of direction that He expects us to figure out before we do anything? And the answer is no. Yes, God has a specific plan for our lives. And yes, we can be assured that He works things for our good in Christ Jesus. And yes, looking back we will often be able to trace God's hand in bringing us to where we are. But while we are free to ask God for wisdom, He does not burden us with the task of divining His will of direction for our lives ahead of time.

The second half of that last sentence is crucial. God does have a specific plan for our lives, *but* it is not one that He expects us to figure out before we make a decision. I'm not saying God won't help you make decisions (it's called wisdom, and we'll talk about it in chapter 8). I'm not saying God doesn't care about your future. I'm not saying God isn't directing your path and in control amidst the chaos of your life. I believe in providence with all my heart. What I am saying is that we should stop thinking of God's will like a corn maze, or a tightrope, or a bull's-eye, or a choose-your-own-adventure novel.

When I was a kid, I loved to read choose-your-own-adventure stories. You'd get to a turning point in the story and if you wanted to flee the country, you'd turn to page 23; and if you wanted to hide out in the cave, you'd turn to page 36. And, oops, the cave turns out to be the side of a volcano, and you die. You made the wrong choice. Fun books for little boys, but not so much fun if that's how God's will works. Many of us fear we'll take the wrong job, or buy the wrong house, or declare the wrong major, or marry the wrong person, and suddenly our lives will blow up. We'll be out of God's will, doomed to spiritual, relational, and physical failure. Or, to put it in Christianese, we'll find ourselves out of "the center of God's will." We'll miss God's best and have to settle for an alternate ending to our lives.

Several years ago I read *The Will of God as a Way of Life*, by Gerald Sittser. His book helped me crystallize my understanding of what I felt was wrong with the traditional understanding of God's will. Here's Sittser's explanation of the usual, and misguided, way of looking at God's will.

> Conventional understanding of God's will defines it as a specific pathway we should follow into the future. God knows what this pathway is, and he has laid it out for us to follow. Our responsibility is to discover this pathway—God's plan for our lives. We

must discover which of the many pathways we could follow is the one we should follow, the one God has planned for us. If and when we make the right choice, we will receive his favor, fulfill our divine destiny and succeed in life. . . . If we choose rightly, we will experience his blessing and achieve success and happiness. If we choose wrongly, we may lose our way, miss God's will for our lives, and remain lost forever in an incomprehensible maze.[2]

This conventional understanding is the wrong way to think of God's will. In fact, expecting God to reveal some hidden will of direction is an invitation to disappointment and indecision. Trusting in God's will of decree is good. Following His will of desire is obedient. Waiting for God's will of direction is a mess. It is bad for your life, harmful to your sanctification, and allows too many Christians to be passive tinkerers who strangely feel more spiritual the less they actually do.

God is not a Magic 8-Ball we shake up and peer into whenever we have a decision to make. He is a good God who gives us brains, shows us the way of obedience, and invites us to take risks for Him. We know God has a plan for our lives. That's wonderful. The problem is we think He's going to tell us the wonderful plan before it unfolds. We feel like we can know—and need to know—what God wants every step of the way. But such preoccupation with finding God's will, as well-intentioned as the desire may be, is more folly than freedom.

The better way is the biblical way: Seek first the kingdom of God, and then trust that He will take care of our needs, even before we know what they are and where we're going.

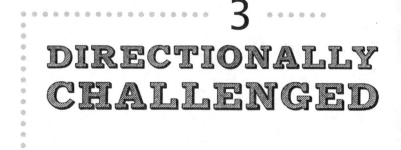

3
DIRECTIONALLY CHALLENGED

Why are so many Christians desperate to find out God's plan for their lives? Why are publishers still willing to crank out will of God books (like this one!) even though there are a bazillion other ones on the market? Why do millions of Christians in this country spend buckets of time and energy waiting for the will of God to be revealed? And why do we fret about the will of God like it's some nuclear warhead pointing at our future happiness?

Let me suggest five reasons.

WE WANT TO PLEASE GOD

Over the years I've talked with many earnest believers who sincerely want to know, "Is this where I'm supposed to be? Is this what I'm supposed to be doing?" These men and women love the Lord. They aren't trying to be difficult. They believe

God has a path picked out for them, and they don't want to miss it and let Him down. If the Lord thinks we should move to Nashville, we don't want to wind up in Fargo. If we're supposed to major in chemical engineering, we don't want to study Russian literature. If we were meant for the mission field, we don't want to land in suburbia.

This is the first reason we seek to know God's specific will of direction for us: We want to please Him. We want to do what God wants. That's good. But as I've already explained and will flesh out in the coming chapters, this is not how the will of God works. We may have the best of intentions in trying to discern God's will, but we should really stop putting ourselves through the misery of overspiritualizing every decision. Our misdirected piety makes following God more mysterious than it was meant to be.

SOME OF US ARE TIMID

The second reason some of us seek God's will of direction is because we are, by nature, quite timid. The entrepreneurial go-getter types may be less inclined to fret over God's will than the deliberate, cautious types. Some Christians need encouragement to think before they act. Others need encouragement to act after they think.

I've known impetuous Christians, but in my personal experience I've seen more who are paralyzed by indecision and inactivity. They refuse to make a decision without all the facts and an almost complete assurance that everything will turn out fine. They quit Pop Warner Football as kids because they might not be the best. They'd rather slack off in school and do poorly by not trying than try and not live up to expectations. These may be the sort of Christians Paul had in mind when he told the Thessalonians to "admonish the idle, encourage the fainthearted, help the weak, be patient with them all" (1 Thessalonians 5:14).[1]

Some Christians have the best intentions in seeking out God's will. They are just too cautious and a little fainthearted. Such Christians need admonition, but they also deserve our patience and help.

WE WANT PERFECT FULFILLMENT

The third reason we seek God's will for direction is we are searching for perfect fulfillment in life. Many of us have had it so good that we have started looking for heaven on earth. We have lost any sort of pilgrim attitude. It's all a matter of perspective. If you think that God has promised this world will be a five-star hotel, you will be miserable as you live though the normal struggles of life. But if you remember that God promised we would be pilgrims and this world may feel more like a desert or even a prison, you might find your life surprisingly happy.

Faith in Jesus does not guarantee that everything will go our way. Look at Hebrews 11, the chapter sometimes called the faith hall of fame. Consider just the first three heroes mentioned in that chapter. As Bible commentator Bruce Waltke has pointed out, Abel had faith and he died; Enoch had faith and he did not die; Noah had faith and everyone else died![2] So just having faith doesn't guarantee your life—or the lives of those around you—will be all candy canes and lollipops. Life isn't always fun, and we shouldn't expect it to be.

Some of this is a generational thing. After all, my peers and I were among the first ones to experience grade inflation, where we got A's for excavating our feelings and "doing our best" at calculus. We were among the first to be programmed for self-esteem, as we learned that having a pulse made us wonderfully special. For as long as we can remember, we've been destined for superstardom.

> We want it all—all we need is for God to show us the way.

Some of us have been prepped for elite schooling since before we could use the potty, and we've been on the traveling soccer teams before we knew not to touch the ball with our hands. We've been stuffed full of praise for mediocrity and had our foibles diagnosed away with hyphenated jargon and pop psychology.

It's no wonder we expect people to affirm us for everything, criticize us for nothing, and pay us for anything we want to do. We figure we should be able to find a great job right out of college in a great location that provides the same standard of living our parents have right now, and involves us in the world's troubles in a way that would make Bono proud. We want it all—all we need is for God to show us the way.

By and large, my grandparents' generation expected much less out of family life, a career, recreation, and marriage. Granted, this sometimes made them unreflective and allowed for quietly dismal marriages. But my generation is on the opposite end of the spectrum. When we marry, we expect great sex, an amazing family life, recreational adventure, cultural experiences, and personal fulfillment at work. It would be a good exercise to ask your grandparents sometimes if they felt fulfilled in their careers. They'll probably look at you as if you're speaking a different language, because you are. Fulfillment was not their goal. Food was, and faithfulness too. Most older folks would probably say something like, "I never thought about fulfillment. I had a job. I ate. I lived. I raised my family. I went to church. I was thankful."

Recently, I was talking with Grandpa DeYoung, a lifelong Christian now in his eighties. I asked him if he ever thought about what God's will was for his life. "I don't think so," was his short response. "God's will was never a question presented to me or I ever thought about. I always felt that my salvation . . . depended on my accepting by faith the things that we believe. After that, I don't think I ever had a problem thinking: 'Is this the right thing for me?'"

The more my grandpa and I talked, the more I realized the will of God beyond trying to obey His moral will was an unfamiliar concept to him. "You just . . . do things" seemed to be my grandpa's sentiment, and as you're doing them and walking with the Lord, you don't spend oodles of time trying to figure out if you like what you are doing. I guess if you keep busy and work your whole life, you don't have time to worry about being fulfilled.

I'm not trying to squash all your hopes and dreams—really. I'm all for big risk-taking dreams (as you'll read shortly). I'm not against people leaving their unhappy jobs to take a shot at what they really love. But as a counterweight to the "make your dreams come true" stuff of graduation speeches, we need the firm reminder that many of us expect too much out of life. We've assumed that we'll experience heaven on earth, and then we get disappointed when earth seems so unheavenly. We have little longing left for our reward in the next life because we've come to expect such rewarding experiences in this life. And when *every* experience and situation *must* be rewarding and put us on the road to complete fulfillment, then suddenly the decisions about where we live, what house we buy, what dorm we're in, and whether we go with tile or laminate take on weighty significance. There is just too much riding on every decision. I'm pretty sure most of us would be more fulfilled if we didn't fixate on fulfillment quite so much.

WE HAVE TOO MANY CHOICES

Of the five reasons for our obsession with finding God's will, this may be the most crucial: *We have too many choices.* I'm convinced that previous generations did not struggle like we do trying to discover God's will because they didn't have as many choices. In many ways, our preoccupation with the will of God is a Western, middle-class phenomenon of the last fifty years. People living on a dollar a day just don't have that many choices to make. Neither did most of our grandparents, let alone their grandparents. A century ago, for the most part, you lived in the place you were born. You did what your mom or dad did, probably worked on the farm if you were a man, and raised kids (and worked on the farm) if you were a woman. Many of the old people I talk to started working when they were young teenagers, and they did anything they could find. They worked for their uncle or dad or started helping with harvest or whatever work was available in town. Ironically, they got more done because they didn't have as many things they could do.

I imagine the choices were much simpler in other areas as well. A century ago, you would have married one of a dozen or so nonrelated eligible young people in town. Even wealthier folks were still bound by location (because of the difficulty of travel) and tradition (because of cultural values and family heritage) in a way that significantly limited their choices. It used to be that young people felt more of a sense of duty to family, citizenship, and church. But now few of us can imagine voluntarily limiting our independence and curtailing our options for something as antiquated as duty.

The result is an endless stream of opportunities. Today we can go to school anywhere, major in hundreds of things, live almost anyplace, have a chance to personally meet thousands of single people in person and millions more on the Internet. We have a gaggle of stores to choose from, dozens of restaurants, hundreds of careers, and millions of choices.

In *The Paradox of Choice*, Barry Schwartz tells of a trip to his local moderately sized grocery store. He found 285 varieties of cookies, 13 sports drinks, 65 box drinks, 85 kids' juices, 75 iced teas, 95 types of chips and pretzels, 15 kinds of bottled water, 80 different pain relievers, 40 options for toothpaste, 150 lipsticks, 360 types of shampoo, 90 different cold remedies, 230 soups, 75 instant gravies, 275 varieties of cereal, 64 types of barbeque sauce, and 22 types of frozen waffles.[3] Anyone who has ever shopped for groceries in North America knows that this list is only a tiny fraction of all the options found in every aisle. That's why we stick with certain cereals or brands or meals because we simply don't have the time or energy to make new choices every time we venture off to the Super Walmart or Safeway. It's also why my wife sends me with a very detailed list in the unfortunate event that I am responsible for the grocery shopping during the week. If she tells me to get baby food, with no further instructions, I could come back with anything from liquid peas to dissolvable, cherry-flavored wagon wheels. I need specifics because there are just too many ways I can screw things up.

In some countries, people suffer from too few choices. In America, we have too many. I remember a missionary from Turkey telling me, tongue in cheek, that one of the hardest parts of being back in the United States was all the salad dressing. "Just get some dressing," he said while we were eating out for lunch. "Don't make me choose among seven different kinds of ranch." My hunch is that most of our obsession with knowing the will of God is due to the fact that we are overburdened with choice. We think choice makes us happy, but there comes a point (and most of us are well past it) where we would actually be better off with fewer choices.

Professor Schwartz's observations about college students are telling, and from my experience, spot-on. He observes that the students he teaches have multiple interests and capabilities. They have gobs of talent and opportunities. The world is wide open to them. But instead of reveling in this freedom, most find it agonizing. They are forced to navigate between competing interests: making money and making a difference, challenging their minds and channeling their creativity, focusing on a career and leaving time for a family, settling down now and traveling abroad for a while, starting a career and trying another internship, living in a bustling city and resting in a pastoral location, going to work right away and going on for more schooling.

If you are a college student, the choices *are* mind boggling. And with friends and family often scattered all over the country or even the world, you have fewer obligations and close relationships to limit your freedom and nothing to anchor you to a vocational tradition or location. Add to this the ability to travel easily and work many jobs by computer from anywhere you like, and the result is massive un-rootedness and an explosion of choice. Everything is up for grabs.

Schwartz summarizes it well:

One quickly learns that "What are you going to do when you graduate?" is not a question many students are eager to hear, let alone answer. It is hard to avoid the conclusion that my students might be better off with a little less talent or with a little more of a sense that they owed it to their families to settle down back home, or even a dose of Depression-era necessity—take the secure job and get on with it! With fewer options and more constraints, many trade-offs would be eliminated, and there would be less self-doubt, less of an effort to justify decisions, more satisfaction, and less second-guessing of the decisions once made.[4]

Schwartz's assessment is dead-on. I'm sure that some people serve the Lord well as they buzz around the world for six months at a time. And I'm sure some young folks are making a difference for Christ as they float from job to job and place to place. But I'm equally certain that many of these same individuals are actually making self-centered decisions in the name of experience, cultural diversity, and sometimes, I hate to say it, under the guise of short-term missions. As a pastor at a university church, I understand that people come and go through our services all the time. That's part of life with grads and undergrads. I like the excitement of new people arriving every year. But if no one settled down and no one stayed put for awhile, let alone a lifetime, we could not minister to all the students in the way we do. The church needs lifers and those who can be counted on for the long haul.

My fear is that of all the choices people face today, the one they rarely consider is, "How can I serve most effectively and fruitfully in the local church?" I wonder if the abundance of opportunities to explore today is doing less to help make well-rounded disciples of Christ and more to help Christians avoid long-term responsibility and have less long-term impact.

With so many choices, it's no surprise that we are always thinking about the greener grass on the other side of the fence. We are always pondering what could be better or what might be nicer about something or someone new. "Decide" comes from the Latin word *decidere*, meaning "to cut off," which explains why decisions are so hard these

> Let's not spiritualize our inability to make decisions in the quest to discover God's will.

days. We can't stand the thought of cutting off any of our options. If we choose A, we feel the sting of not having B and C and D. As a result, every choice feels worse than no choice at all. And when we do make an important choice, we end up with buyers' remorse, wondering if we are settling for second best. Or, worse yet, we end up living in our parents' basement indefinitely as we try to find ourselves and hear God's voice. Our freedom to do anything and go anywhere ends up feeling like bondage more than liberty, because decision making feels like pain, not pleasure.

Too many young people today have no stability, no certainty, no predictability, little decisiveness, and lots of self-doubt. It takes longer and longer for people to settle down. And some never do. I'm not advocating that everyone move back to his hometown and take whatever job is available (though that would be at least a step toward something for some people). Some of you should go overseas and others will move to new places. But I am advocating floundering less, making a difference for God sooner, and—above all—not spiritualizing, year after year, our inability to make decisions in the elusive quest to discover God's will. I'm arguing that our eagerness to know God's will is probably less indicative of a heart desperately wanting to obey God and more about our heads spinning with all the choices to be made.

WE ARE COWARDS

The final reason we want to know the will of God is because we are cowardly. It's true. Sometimes when we pray to know the will of God, we are praying a coward's prayer: "Lord, tell me what to do so nothing bad will happen to me and I won't have to face danger or the unknown." We want to know everything is going to be fine for us or for those we love. But that's not how God spoke to Esther. As a Jewish woman who won an unusual beauty contest to become Xerxes' queen (see Esther 2:2–17), Esther would learn that God's plans can include risk —and an opportunity to show courage.

The king's right-hand man, Haman, was the enemy of the Jews and devised a plot to kill all the Jewish people, and Xerxes, king of Persia, unwittingly signed this decree. When Mordecai, Esther's older cousin and guardian, learned of this plot, he told Esther, knowing she was the only one in a position to save the Jewish people—her people. But she refused, telling him that if she visited King Xerxes without being summoned, she would, by Persian law, be killed—unless the king extended the golden scepter and spared her life. Entering the throne room on her own was very risky, which is why Esther sent people to Mordecai to say that she wouldn't do it.

The Scriptures give us Mordecai's response to the words of Esther's emissaries:

> *Then Mordecai told them to reply to Esther, "Do not think to yourself that in the king's palace you will escape any more than all the other Jews. For if you keep silent at this time, relief and deliverance will rise for the Jews from another place, but you and your father's house will perish. And who knows whether you have not come to the kingdom for such a time as this?"* (Esther 4:13–14)

So what would you do at this point? Pray for some sign from heaven? Wait for God's will to be revealed? Question why God would put you in such a predicament? Do nothing, figuring that anything involving suffering and possible death must not be His plan for your life? Look at what Esther did:

> *Then Esther told them to reply to Mordecai, "Go, gather all the Jews to be found in Susa, and hold a fast on my behalf, and do not eat or drink for three days, night or day. I and my young women will also fast as you do. Then I will go to the king, though it is against the law, and if I perish, I perish."* (vv. 15–16)

Notice what we don't read in this story. We don't read of Esther seeking any divine word from the Lord, though a discerning reader may see God at work in Mordecai's advice to her. She had no promise as to what the future would look like. All she knew was that saving her people was a good thing. God did not tell her what would happen if she obeyed or exactly what she could do to ensure success. She had to take a risk for God. "If I perish, I perish" was her courageous cry.

Esther didn't wait for weeks or months trying to discern God's will for her life before she acted. She simply did what was right and forged ahead without any special word from God. If the king extended to her the golden scepter, praise the Lord. If he did not, she died.

Esther was more man than most men I know, myself included. Many of us—men and women—are extremely passive and cowardly. We don't take risks for God because we are obsessed with safety, security, and most of all, with the future. That's why most of our prayers fall into one of two categories. Either we ask that everything would be fine or we ask to know that everything will be fine. We pray for health, travel, jobs—and we should pray for these things. But a lot of prayers boil down to, "God, don't let anything unpleasant happen to anyone. Make everything in the world nice for everyone." And when we aren't praying this kind of prayer, we are praying for God to tell us that everything will turn out fine.

> His way is not a crystal ball. His way is wisdom.

That's often what we are asking for when we pray to know the will of God. We aren't asking for holiness, or righteousness, or an awareness of sin. We want God to tell us what to do so everything will turn out pleasant for us. "Tell me who to marry, where to live, what school to go to, what job to take. Show me the future so I won't have to take any risks." This doesn't sound much like Esther.

Obsessing over the future is not how God wants us to live, because showing us the future is not God's way. His way is to speak to us in the Scriptures and transform us by the renewing of our minds. His way is not a crystal ball. His way is wisdom. We should stop looking for God to reveal the future to us and remove all risk from our lives. We should start looking to God—His character and His promises—and thereby have confidence to take risks for His name's sake.

God is all-knowing and all-powerful. He has planned out and works out every detail of our lives—the joyous days and the difficult—all for our good (Ecclesiastes 7:14). Because we have confidence in God's will of decree, we can radically commit ourselves to His will of desire, without fretting over a hidden will of direction.

In other words, God doesn't take risks, so we can.

For some this means trusting God enough to let your money slip through your fingers. For others it means holding fast to the Word of God in some difficult circumstances or an unpopular situation. For others it means cross-cultural missions, or more evangelism, or a new dream, or confession of sin, or confrontation of sin, or new vulnerability in a relationship. And for some it means getting off your duff and getting a job, or overcoming your fear of rejection and pursuing a lovely Christian woman. For all of us it means putting aside our insatiable desire to have every aspect of our lives, or even the most important aspects of our lives, nailed down before our eyes before we get there.

> We can stop pleading with God to show us the future [being] confident that He holds the future.

God has a wonderful plan for your life—a plan that will take you through trial and triumph as you are transformed into the image of His Son (Romans 8:28–29). Of this we can be absolutely confident. But God's normal way of operation is not to show this plan to us ahead of time—in retrospect, maybe; in advance, rarely.

Are you feeling directionally challenged by this? Don't despair. God promises to be your sun and your shield and to carry you and protect with His strong right arm. So we can stop pleading with God to show us the future, and start living and obeying like we are confident that He holds the future.

OUR MAGIC 8-BALL GOD

The conventional approach to the will of God—where God's will is like a corn maze with only one way out and lots of dead ends, or like a bull's-eye with the center of God's will in the middle and second best everywhere else, or like a Magic 8-Ball that we are supposed to shake around until some generic answer floats to the top—is not helpful. It is not good for our decision making. It is not good for our sanctification. And sometimes it is frankly dishonoring to Christ.

In chapter 3 I mentioned some reasons we are obsessed with knowing this supposed will of direction. In this chapter I want to talk more directly about why this conventional approach to the will of God is wrong, and then in the next chapter we'll look at Matthew 6:25–34 and consider a better way.

Before we get there, I want to highlight five problems with the conventional approach to the will of God.[1]

WE TEND TO FOCUS ON
NONMORAL DECISIONS

First, the conventional approach to discovering God's will focuses almost all of our attention on nonmoral decisions. Scripture does not tell us whether we should live in Minnesota or Maine. It does not tell us whether we should go to Michigan State University or Wheaton College. It does not tell us whether we should buy a house or rent an apartment. It does not tell us whether we should marry a wonderful Christian named Tim or some other wonderful Christian guy. Scripture does not tell us what to do this summer or what job to take or where to go to grad school.

Once, while preaching on this topic, I said in a bold declarative statement, "God doesn't care where you go to school or where you live or what job you take." A thoughtful young woman talked to me afterward and was discouraged to hear that God didn't care about the most important decisions in her life. I explained to her that I probably wasn't very clear. God certainly cares about these decisions insofar as He cares for us and every detail of our lives. But in another sense, and this was the point I was trying to make, these are not the most important issues in God's book. The most important issues for God are moral purity, theological fidelity, compassion, joy, our witness, faithfulness, hospitality, love, worship, and faith. These are His big concerns. The problem is that we tend to focus most of our attention on everything else. We obsess over the things God has not mentioned and may never mention, while, by contrast, we spend little time on all the things God has already revealed to us in the Bible.

In other words, we spend most of our time trying to figure out nonethical decisions. When I say nonethical or nonmoral matters, I'm talking about decisions between two or more options, none of which is forbidden in Scripture. Choosing between a career in biology and a career in politics is a nonethical decision, provided—and this is a big proviso—that your motives are right and what you'll be doing is right. So if your career in medicine means you work as a doctor who performs abortions, that would be wrong, as would a career in politics in which you slander and cheat your way to the top. But if you are motivated by right and doing right, then your career choice is not a moral decision. The Bible simply does not address every decision we must make.

Of course, this doesn't mean we shouldn't be thoughtful in choosing a career, nor that we should ignore how God has wired us or the command to do all to the glory of God (1 Corinthians 10:31). My point is that we should spend more time trying to figure out how to act justly, love mercy, and walk humbly with God (as instructed in Micah 6:8) as a doctor or lawyer and less time worrying about whether God wants us to be a doctor or lawyer.

DO WE HAVE A SNEAKY GOD?

Second, the conventional approach implies that we have a sneaky God. In the usual understanding of God's will, God knows what we should do. He has the perfect plan for our lives. And He'll hold us accountable if we don't follow His will. But He won't show us what that will is. The traditional approach to God's will makes God into a tricky little deity who plays hide and seek with us.

Just to be clear, God does not hide things from His people. There are lots of scenarios we don't know, lots of mysteries we can't figure out. There is a will of decree that is not usually known to the people of God (Deuteronomy 29:29). But He is not trying to confuse us or hide truth. In the conventional view of God's will, however, we get the impression that He not only hides His will from us, but He then *expects* us to find it. So we obsess over God's will of direction, eventually getting frustrated with God for not showing us what He wants. We end up disappointed with ourselves or angry with God because we can't seem to figure out how to find God's will for our lives.

> Anxiety is simply living out the future before it gets here.

I NEED TO KNOW THE FUTURE

Third, the conventional approach encourages a preoccupation with the future. The way many Christians treat God's will is no different than you might treat a horoscope. We come to God and we want to know, "Is the job market good for Kevin today? Will I find my true love? Should I live in states that start with the letter A?" Our fascination with the will of God often betrays our lack of trust in God's promises and provision.

We don't just want His word that He will be with us; we want Him to show us the end from the beginning and prove to us that He can be trusted. We want to know what tomorrow will bring instead of being content with simple obedience on the journey.

And so we obsess about the future and we get anxious, because anxiety, after all, is simply living out the future before it gets here. But listen to what James says:

> *Come now, you who say, "Today or tomorrow we will go into such and such a town and spend a year there and trade and make a profit"—yet you do not know what tomorrow will bring. What is your life? For you are a mist that appears for a little time and then vanishes. Instead you ought to say, "If the Lord wills, we will live and do this or that." (James 4:13–15)*

This is one of the clearest texts on the sovereignty of God. If we make it to the grocery store this afternoon, according to James, the Lord willed it. If we live to be a hundred, the Lord willed it. If we live to be only forty-five, the Lord willed it. We don't have to say "If the Lord wills" after every sentence, but it must be in our heads and hearts. We must live our lives believing that all of our plans and strategies are subject to the immutable will of God. Therefore, we should be humble in looking to the future because we don't control it; God does.

And we should be hopeful in looking to the future because God controls it, not us.

This brings us back to anxiety, our tendency to live out the future before it arrives. We must renounce our sinful desire to know the future and to be in control. We are not gods. We walk by faith, not by sight. We risk because God does not risk. We walk into the future in God-glorifying confidence, not because the future is known to us but because it is known to God. And that's all we need to know. Worry about the future is not simply a character tic, it is the sin of unbelief, an indication that our hearts are not resting in the promises of God.

DON'T BLAME ME!

Fourth, the conventional approach undermines personal responsibility, accountability, and initiative. Let me give an example of what I mean by the conventional approach to the will of God undermining personal responsibility. When I got the call to come to be the senior pastor at University Reformed Church, I was happily serving as an associate pastor in northwest Iowa. It was a hard decision to come to a new church and leave a church I loved. Some people in Iowa were angry about my decision. It would have been very easy to say to people (because I've heard lines like it before): "I love being in Iowa. If it were up to me, I would stay here. It doesn't make a lot of human sense for me to go. But as I've prayed, it's been very clear to me that this is what the Lord wants. I'm not sure I even like it. But I feel very strongly that it's God will for me to go to East Lansing."

That could have gotten people off my case, but it would have been unfair. It wasn't God's fault I was leaving. My wife and I prayed to God a lot about the decision, and I think it was a decision that pleased Him, just like He would have been pleased if we had stayed. But it was my decision. I was responsible for leaving. I chose. I decided. Yes, in the ultimate sense God already had it decided; that's always true. But it would have been wrong for me to use God's will as a way to remove my personal responsibility in the decision.

> "It seems like the Lord is leading" is a better way of communicating our dependence on God than "God told me so."

The same is true of personal accountability. We need to be careful that we aren't using God as the trump card in all our decisions. Just because you pray doesn't mean your decisions are beyond objection. I know some people talk about God's work in their lives using different phrases. But if we say "*God* told me to do this" or "*God's* leading me here," this puts our decisions out of reach from criticisms or concerns. We should choose some different terminology. "I prayed about it, and this seems best" or "It seems like the Lord is leading" would be a more helpful way of communicating our dependence on God. We don't want "God told me so" or "God laid it on my heart" or "It's God's will" or worse yet, "God told me that He wants you to do such and such" to be conversation stoppers that remove accountability in decision making.

I'll never forget my poor beleaguered roommate talking with me after he took a risk and told a nice young lady that he liked her. They went on a long walk. He was pretty sure she would reciprocate his declaration of affection. But it turned out she wasn't interested. She was a sweet girl, a good Christian. She didn't mean to have bad theology. But instead of just saying "I'm not interested" or "I don't like you" or "Quit stalking me" or something, she went all spiritual on him. "I've been praying a lot about you," she demurred, "and the Holy Spirit told me no." "No?" my confused roommate asked. "No . . . never," she replied.

Poor guy—he got rejected, not only by this sweet girl, but by the Holy Spirit. The third person of the Trinity took a break from pointing people to Jesus to tell this girl not to date my roommate. I didn't know that was in the Spirit's job description. But I bet at any Christian school there are scores of men and women blaming God for their breakups.

Whether it's the Holy Spirit saying "No, never" or Jesus apparently wanting to "date" a myriad of girls at every campus,[2] God's will is frequently employed as an excuse for difficult relationship decisions. This is the sort of accountability-dodging jargon we want to avoid. If you aren't interested in dating or courtship or marriage or whatever, just say "No thanks" or "Not now," but please don't make God the bad guy in your relational messes.

The conventional approach also undermines personal initiative. Haddon Robinson explains:

If we ask, "How can I know the will of God?" we may be asking the wrong question. The Scriptures do not command us to find God's will for most of life's choices nor do we have any passage instructing on how it can be determined. Equally significant, the Christian community has never agreed on how God provides us with such special revelation. Yet we persist in searching for God's will because decisions require thought and sap energy. We seek relief from the responsibility of decision-making and we feel less threatened by being passive rather than active when making important choices.[3]

Does this mean that God's Word has nothing to say about how we live our lives and make decisions? Of course not. But when it comes to most of our daily decisions, and even a lot of life's "big" decisions, God expects and encourages us to make choices, confident that He's already determined how to fit our choices into His sovereign will. Passivity is a plague among Christians. It's not just that we don't do anything; it's that we feel spiritual for not doing anything. We imagine that our inactivity is patience and sensitivity to God's leading. At times it may be; but it's also quite possible we are just lazy. When we hyper-spiritualize our decisions, we can veer off into impulsive and foolish decisions. But more likely as Christians we fall into endless patterns of vacillation, indecision, and regret. No doubt, selfish ambition is a danger for Christians, but so is complacency, listless wandering, and passivity that pawns itself off as spirituality. Perhaps our inactivity is not so much waiting on God as it is an expression of the fear of man, the love of the praise of man, and disbelief in God's providence.

IT'S SUBJECTIVE

Fifth, the conventional approach enslaves us in the chains of hopeless subjectivism. Don't misunderstand me. Our decisions are subjective sometimes. That's not always bad. Sometimes we go on a hunch or an intuition or a feeling. It's not necessarily bad to make nonmoral decisions based on our gut or feelings. What's bad is when we are slaves to this kind of subjectivism. So we never take risks because we never feel peace about them. Or we second-guess our decisions because we feel uneasy about them. The fact is, most big decisions in life leave us feeling a little unsettled. They are, after all, big decisions. When you decide to get married or move or buy a house, it will be scary because it's big and new and unknown and permanent (at least the marriage should be). But this doesn't mean the Lord's withholding peace about the decision in order to get you to back out.

I'm not saying subjective decisions are wrong. We make decisions based on a "feeling" all the time. But a subjective divining of God's will should not be your decision-making process. It's a dead-end street. How do you know when an open door is the Lord's open door or the Devil tempting you? How do you know when a closed door is the Lord's answer to your prayer or the Lord testing your steadfastness and resolve? These are the conundrums people get into when all their decisions come from subjective attempts to discern God's will for their lives.

I recently read a book by a popular Christian author who advocated an approach to intimacy with God that entailed constant checking and rechecking with the Lord regarding the most trivial details in life.[4] I don't wish to impugn his motives or question his emphasis on a close relationship with God, which can be a helpful corrective for some of our stodgy, buttoned-downed brethren. But the book laid out an approach to decision making that made my head spin. We were told to listen for God's voice at every possible fork in the road. Should I send this e-mail? Should I paint the bathroom? Should I stay late at work? Should I go to the ranch or stay home? What book of the Bible should I read this morning? Which chapter? Is this a good day for fishing? Should I go on a hike? Do you want to heal our dog? Should we go on the camping trip? When should we go? (The Lord said April 21–24, by the way.) Should we get a new puppy?

All of these were actual questions asked of the Lord over the course of the book's narrative. Again, I respect the author for wanting to be obedient to God. But why did the Lord give us brains and say so much about gaining wisdom if all we are really supposed to do is call on the Lord to tell us what to do in a thousand different nonmoral decisions?

Besides, I don't recall in the book ever hearing how this divining of God's will actually works, except that we "try on" answers and second-guess ourselves a lot. I couldn't help but feel sorry for the author when he wrote about his horse-riding accident and the regret he lived with after the fact because he asked the Lord *if* he should ride, but he never asked the Lord *where* he should ride. He recalled praying over the horses and feeling "like it wasn't working," but he went out anyway because he just wanted to go for a ride like a normal person. Surely, this is misplaced shame. It's a great idea to pray for safety before saddling up the horse, but that doesn't mean we need to wait for the "all clear" feeling in our bones before we head out. Would God really spare us from all accidents if we simply asked Him enough particulars and prayed hard enough at the start of the day? If something goes bad in our lives, do we really need the added burden of feeling like it all could have been prevented if we had just better discerned God's will? And how do we do His will anyway other than probing some subjective feeling in our gut that inevitably leads to much hand-wringing and second-guessing?

This highlights one of the great ironies about the will-of-God talk among Christians. If there really is a perfect will of God we are meant to discover, in which we will find tremendous freedom and fulfillment, why does it seem that everyone looking for God's will is in such bondage and confusion? Christ died to give us freedom from the law (Galatians 5:1), so why turn the will of God into another law leading to slavery?[5] And, to make matters worse, this law is personalized, invisible, and indecipherable; whereas the Mosaic law (which was hard enough already), was at least objective, public, and understandable. What a burden. Expecting God, through our subjective sense of things, to point the way for *every* decision we face, no matter how trivial, is not only impractical and unrealistic, it is a recipe for disappointment and false guilt. And that's hardly what intimacy with Jesus should be all about.

5

A BETTER WAY?

The question then becomes: Is there a better way to walk in the will of God? The answer is a resounding yes! There is most certainly a better way. It's an old way. It's a biblical way. It's Jesus' way.

Listen to Jesus' explanation of the way of God in the Sermon on the Mount:

> "Therefore I tell you, do not be anxious about your life, what you will eat or what you will drink, nor about your body, what you will put on. Is not life more than food, and the body more than clothing? Look at the birds of the air: they neither sow nor reap nor gather into barns, and yet your heavenly Father feeds them. Are you not of more value than they? And which of you by being anxious can add a single hour to his span of life? And why are you anxious about clothing? Consider the lilies of the field, how they grow: they neither toil nor spin, yet I tell you,

*even Solomon in all his glory was not arrayed like one of these.
But if God so clothes the grass of the field, which today is alive
and tomorrow is thrown into the oven, will he not much more
clothe you, O you of little faith? Therefore do not be anxious, saying, 'What shall we eat?' or 'What shall we drink?' or 'What
shall we wear?' For the Gentiles seek after all these things, and
your heavenly Father knows that you need them all. But seek first
the kingdom of God and his righteousness, and all these things
will be added to you.*

*"Therefore do not be anxious about tomorrow, for tomor-
row will be anxious for itself. Sufficient for the day is its own
trouble."* (Matthew 6:25–34)

DON'T WORRY; SEEK HIS KINGDOM

The big idea of this passage could not be any clearer: Jesus
does not want us to worry about the future. God knows what
we need to live. When He wants us to die, we will die. And as
long as He wants us to live, we will live. He will provide us with
the food, drink, jobs, housing, with everything that we need
to live and glorify Him in this life until He wants us to glorify
Him by dying. Worrying and fretting and obsessing about the
future, even if it is a pseudo-holy worry that attempts to discern
the will of God, will not add one single hour to your life, and
it will certainly not add any happiness or holiness either.

Worry and anxiety are not merely bad habits or idiosyn-
crasies. They are sinful fruits that blossom from the root of unbelief. Jesus doesn't treat obsession with the future as a personal

quirk, but as evidence of little faith (v. 30). Worry and anxiety reflect our hearts' distrust in the goodness and sovereignty of God. Worry is a spiritual issue and must be fought with faith.[1]

We must fight to believe that God has mercy for today's troubles and, no matter what may come tomorrow, that God will have new mercies for tomorrow's troubles (Lamentations 3:22–23). God's way is not to show us what tomorrow looks like or even to tell us what decisions we should

> The question God cares about most is not "Where should I live?" but "Do I love the Lord with all my heart?"

make tomorrow. That's not His way because that's not the way of faith. God's way is to tell us that He knows tomorrow, He cares for us, and therefore, we should not worry.

Verse 33 is crucial for understanding the will of God for our lives. Jesus says, "Seek first the kingdom of God and his righteousness." He doesn't call on us to seek a divine word before scheduling another semester of classes or deciding between bowling and putt-putt golf. He calls us to run hard after Him, His commands, and His glory. The decision to be in God's will is not the choice between Memphis or Fargo or engineering or art; it's the daily decision we face to seek God's kingdom or ours, submit to His lordship or not, live according to His rules or our own. The question God cares about most is not "Where should I live?" but "Do I love the Lord with all my heart, soul, strength, and mind, and do I love my neighbor as myself?" (Luke 10:27) It's that second question that gets to the heart of God's will for your life.

DITTO FOR THE APOSTLE PAUL

The apostle Paul echoes Jesus' message about what the center of God's will is. In fact, in four key passages he uses the phrase "the will of God," "his will" and "the will of the Lord" to describe God's call upon our lives. Walking in God's will means seeking first God's kingdom and His righteousness.

First, God's will is that we live holy, set-apart lives: "For this is the will of God, your sanctification" (1 Thessalonians 4:3).

There you have it in a nutshell—God's will for your life. I love to stand in the pulpit and tell people, "I know exactly what God's will is for your life." They usually look a little perplexed. Then I take them to 1 Thessalonians 4:3. Most people are disappointed when they see my point. They wanted something more concrete than sanctification. But specific step-by-step instruction is not usually how God operates. His way is to show His holiness, declare us holy in Christ, then exhort us to grow in holiness in daily life. That's God's will of desire for you. And that's His will of direction too.

He wants you to buy a house that will make you holy. If you marry, He wants you to get married so you can be holy. He wants you to have a job that will help you grow in holiness. Count on it: God's will is *always* your sanctification. He has set you and me apart that we would grow to be more like Christ.

Second, we are to always rejoice, pray, and give thanks. Paul the apostle gives three straightforward commands: "Rejoice always, pray without ceasing, give thanks in all circumstances; for this is the will of God in Christ Jesus for you" (1 Thessalonians 5:16–18).

These are the things worth pondering and worth our energy and efforts. Don't spend all your time wondering to your friends about whom to marry, where to live, how many kids to have, where to go on vacation, and what job to take. Instead, make sure you are practicing 1 Thessalonians 5:16–18. Are you joyful always? Are you praying continually? Are you giving thanks in all circumstances? You ought to be. For this is God's will for us in Christ Jesus.

Third, we are to know God's will so we can bear fruit and know Him better. "And so, from the day we heard, we have not ceased to pray for you, asking that you may be filled with the knowledge of his will in all spiritual wisdom and understanding" (Colossians 1:9).

Paul prayed that the Colossians would know God's will. So does that mean we should be looking to God to make our decisions for us after all? Look what Paul says next: ". . . so as to walk in a manner worthy of the Lord, fully pleasing to him, bearing fruit in every good work and increasing in the knowledge of God. May you be strengthened with all power, according to his glorious might, for all endurance and patience with joy, giving thanks to the Father, who has qualified you to share in the inheritance of the saints in light" (Colossians 1:10–12). Being filled with the knowledge of God's will doesn't mean getting divine messages about our summer plans and financial investments. It means we bear fruit, grow in our understanding of God, are strengthened with power unto patience, and joyfully give thanks to the Father.

It's about *who* we are, not *where* we are.

Fourth, the will of God is to be filled with the Holy Spirit. "Therefore do not be foolish, but understand what the will of the Lord is" (Ephesians 5:17). Again, we see that understanding the will of God is a good thing. But if we keep reading in Ephesians 5 we'll see that the Lord's will is that we don't get drunk and that we are filled with the Holy Spirit. Which, in turn, means addressing one another in psalms, hymns, and spiritual songs; singing to the Lord with all our hearts; giving thanks always and for everything; and submitting to one another out of reverence for Christ.

So what is the will of God that Paul outlines in these verses? Sittser summarizes it well:

> And what is that will [of God]? Is it some specific, secret plan God has for us and wants us to spend days, weeks, even years discovering? Not at all. Rather it consists of a sober life, living in the power of the Holy Spirit, and offering praise and gratitude to God for his goodness. Paul's main concern is about how believers conduct themselves in ordinary life.[2]

> God never assures us of health, success, or ease. But He promises us something even better, to make us . . . humble like Christ.

Simply put, *God's will is your growth in Christlikeness.* God promises to work all things together for our good that we might be conformed to the image of His Son (Romans 8:28–29). And the degree to which this sounds like a lame promise is the degree to which we prefer the stones and scorpions of this world to the true bread from heaven (Matthew 7:9–11). God never assures us of health, success, or ease. But He promises us something even better: He promises to make us loving, pure, and humble like Christ. In short, God's will is that you and I get happy and holy in Jesus.

So go marry someone, provided you're equally yoked and you actually like being with each other. Go get a job, provided it's not wicked. Go live somewhere in something with somebody or nobody. But put aside the passivity and the quest for complete fulfillment and the perfectionism and the preoccupation with the future, and for God's sake start making some decisions in your life. Don't wait for the liver-shiver. If you are seeking first the kingdom of God and His righteousness, you will be in God's will, so just go out and do something.

The only chains God wants us to wear are the chains of righteousness—not the chains of hopeless subjectivism, not the shackles of risk-free living, not the fetters of horoscope decision making—just the chains befitting a bond servant of Christ Jesus. Die to self. Live for Christ. And then do what you want, and go where you want, for God's glory.

God's will for your life is not very complicated. Obviously, living a Christlike life is hard work, and what following Jesus entails is not clear in every situation. But as an overarching principle, the will of God for your life is pretty straightforward: Be holy like Jesus, by the power of the Spirit, for the glory of God.

6
ORDINARY GUIDANCE and SUPERNATURAL SURPRISES

I have been making the case that God's will is not an unexplained labyrinth whose center we are supposed to discover. God's will for our lives is much simpler than this conventional approach. The will of God for our lives is that we seek first His kingdom and His righteousness. The most important decision we face is the daily decision to live for Christ and die to self.

If we do those two things, then we are free to choose between jobs and schools and locations. God wants us to stop obsessing about the future and trust that He holds the future. We should put aside the passivity and the perfectionism and the quest for perfect fulfillment and get on with our lives. God does not have a specific plan for our lives that He means for us to decipher ahead of time.

At this point, some of you may be saying: "That's nice. I think I agree. This approach to the will of God is freeing. But

I still have tons of choices. Does this mean God won't help in making decisions? Is God just a distant deity, uninvolved in the nitty-gritty details of my life?"

Those are fair questions. They are questions about guidance. So let me be clear: I believe God guides us in decision making. But note the key word there: "God *guides* us in decision making." I did not say, "God expects us to discover His plan for our lives." The difference between the two sentences is huge. We are not talking about how God reveals to us ahead of time every decision we must make in life. Yes it's proper for Christians to pray to God and seek wisdom from God when we face decisions, even nonethical decisions. That's not a bad idea. What *is* a bad idea is treating nonethical decisions as weightier than they really are because you think that there is One Right Answer that you must discover.

HOW DOES GOD GUIDE?

What's also a bad idea is expecting God to tell us what to do whenever we are perplexed. Hebrews 1:1–2 is a key text for understanding how God speaks to us in the new covenant: "Long ago, at many times and in many ways, God spoke to our fathers by the prophets, but in these last days he has spoken to us by his Son, whom he appointed the heir of all things, through whom also he created the world."

These two verses, read in the context of the rest of Hebrews, give us valuable insight into how God guides His people. God can speak to people in many ways, the writer explains, but His full and complete revelation is now spoken by His Son, Jesus Christ. As we'll see from the opening chapters of Hebrews, God speaking by His Son includes not only divine revelation in the person of Christ—that is, Jesus shows us what God is like—but also divine revelation through the Spirit of Christ speaking in the Scriptures.

Perhaps this seems a little confusing, so let me try to make my argument in a step-by-step sequence. Leaning on the book *Guidance and the Voice of God* by Phillip Jensen and Tony Payne,[1] I will offer five statements to help us understand God's guidance in the book of Hebrews.

Statement 1: God guides us by His invisible providence at all times. This is another way of stating Ephesians 1:11: "[God] works all things according to the counsel of his will." God has you where you are for a reason. He has given you success this week for a reason. He has sent hardship into your life this week for a reason. In everything, the invisible hand of providence is lovingly directing your life—behind the scenes—down to the smallest detail. We often assume that guidance means God whispers secret plans in our ears. But we would be less anxious to get special revelatory guidance if we thought more about God's providential guidance by which He sovereignly directs our affairs at all times.

Statement 2: God can speak to His people in many different ways, guiding them with their conscious cooperation. The first statement speaks of guidance behind the scenes, guidance that we aren't aware of and don't sense until we look back on things later. This second statement is talking about a different kind of guidance—not the invisible hand of providence, but the voice of God communicating with us and directing us by our conscious cooperation. Hebrews 1 says God has spoken to His people in many different ways. He spoke to our biblical ancestors by a still small voice, by angels, by dreams, by inner promptings, by the mouth of a donkey, by a burning bush, by writing on a wall. God has shown Himself capable of guiding His people and communicating with them in various ways.

Statement 3: In these last days, God has spoken to us by His Son. The book of Hebrews is an extended argument for the supremacy and superiority of Jesus Christ. He is superior to angels, superior to Levitical high priests, superior to the blood of bulls and goats, and superior to other ways of revelation. God can speak to His people in many ways. But in these last days, which were inaugurated with the supernatural events of the cross, resurrection, and Pentecost, God has spoken to us by means of His supreme and superior revelation, Jesus Christ.

What does it mean that God now speaks to us by His Son? It means that God shows His own person and character in the face of Christ. Jesus "is the radiance of the glory of God and the exact imprint of his nature" (Hebrews 1:3). It also means that salvation has been accomplished in the Son. God's judgment on sin can be seen in His judgment on Christ. The cross speaks a loud word of God's mercy for sinners. And when Hebrews says "in these last days [God] has spoken to us by His Son" (1:2), it also means that now God's word to us is centered on Jesus. God spoke through the life, death, resurrection, and the teachings of Jesus. And God spoke through the apostles and their associates who were commissioned to testify about Jesus.

Statement 4: God continues to speak to us by His Son through His Spirit in the Scriptures. When Hebrews was written, Jesus Christ was no longer speaking audibly in person. Jesus had already died, rose again, and ascended to heaven. Jesus could no longer be seen. You could not meet with Him face-to-face. But He was still speaking. So how?

Hebrews operates under the assumption that the Son's speaking takes place through the Spirit in the Scriptures. The theology of Hebrews is rooted in the Old Testament. In fact, there are several mini-commentaries on Old Testament texts: Psalm 2 in Hebrews 2, Psalm 110 in Hebrews 5–7, Jeremiah 31 in Hebrews 8–9, Psalm 40 in Hebrews 10, and Psalm 95 in Hebrews 3–4. In these two chapters (Hebrews 3 and 4), the author is warning against unbelief. And so the writer quotes from Psalm 95: "Today, if you hear his voice, do not harden your hearts as [you did in the rebellion]" (vv. 7–8).

It may be a good idea to open the Bible for yourself at this point so you can see how the author of Hebrews uses this Old Testament text. In Hebrews 3:7, the author writes, "Therefore, as the Holy Spirit says," and then he quotes from Psalm 95. Remarkably, this word of Scripture, written a thousand years prior, can be introduced with the words "the Holy Spirit says." Scripture is not a dead letter. God not only *has spoken* in the Scriptures, but he *continues to speak* through the Scriptures. That's the assumption behind Hebrews 3:7.

The rest of Hebrews 3, and continuing into chapter 4, is nothing but a commentary on Psalm 95. The psalm is quoted again in 3:15 and 4:3 and in 4:7, where the author says for the third time, "Today, if you hear his voice, do not harden your hearts." And where do we hear this voice? That's the question that concerns us. We've already seen that God speaks through His Son in these last days, and that the Holy Spirit still speaks in the Scriptures, and now we receive further confirmation that God continues to speak in the Bible.

> Apart from the Spirit working through Scripture, God does not promise to use any other means to guide us.

Thus Hebrews 4:12, which brings this little commentary on Psalm 95 to a close, says, "For the word of God is living and active. Sharper than any double-edged sword, it penetrates even to dividing soul and spirit, joints and marrow; it judges the thoughts and attitudes of the heart" (NIV).

So the argument in Hebrews 1–4 goes like this: (1) God can speak in many ways. (2) In these last days, God has spoken by his Son. (3) God speaks to us by His Son through the Holy Spirit speaking by the living and active Word of God. Which brings us to the last statement concerning God's guidance.

Statement 5: Apart from the Spirit working through Scripture, God does not promise to use any other means to guide us, nor should we expect him to. When we read the Bible, we know we are hearing from God. We are not only reading what God has inspired by the Spirit, but what He continues to say by the same Spirit. By contrast, hearing from God outside the Bible in these last days is always more tenuous, less clear, and less authoritative. We have no promise in Scripture that God will speak to us apart from the Spirit speaking through His Word.

DON'T EXPECT THE UNEXPECTED

"But wait just a minute," someone might say. "God seems to be more creative than you give Him credit for. Even if we figure that the Old Testament was a different era, what about the Holy Spirit dwelling in us? Doesn't He guide us? And what about the book of Acts? Don't we see God showing up in miraculous events and speaking to His people in surprising ways?"

Our imaginary questioner has a point. Just look at the book of Acts. We read of numerous visions—a vision to Ananias (9:10–16), a vision of unclean animals (10:10–17), a vision of a man of Macedonia (16:6–10), a vision in Corinth (18:9), and a vision on the road to Damascus (22:17–21). And we read of angels appearing to Philip (8:26), Peter (12:7–8), and Paul (27:23). There are examples of audible voices (9:3–6; 10:13, 15, 19–20; 23:11), and mysterious promptings to go somewhere (8:29; 20:22–23), and a prediction about the future from the prophet Agabus (21:10–11). It seems like God shows up and tells people where to go and guides them by means other than the Spirit speaking through the Scriptures.

But there are a couple of considerations that make me think these examples in Acts are not meant to be the normal pattern for our lives. First, it's important to realize that these events of special revelation weren't normal even for the apostles. Take

Paul, for example. On occasion, God directly told him to go somewhere, but most of the time Paul made decisions like the rest of us. He used rather tentative phrases like, "It seemed good to the Holy Spirit and to us" (Acts 15:28–29). In almost every case, he simply decided where to go and how to get there (Acts 20:16). In 1 Corinthians 16 he laid out his plans very prosaically, basically saying, "When I arrive, I will make introductions. Then some people will accompany me, if that seems good. Once I've gone through Macedonia, I will come to you. I'll stay awhile, maybe even the winter. I want to take my time if the Lord permits. Then I'll go on to Ephesus because there is a good opportunity there."

> With few exceptions, Paul . . . made his own decisions about the nonmoral matters of his life.

You don't get the sense that the apostle got angelic visits every other day and waited for his dreams to tell him what to do. With few exceptions, Paul planned, strategized, and made his own decisions about the nonmoral matters of his life.

Second, when we look carefully at the instances of special revelation in the book of Acts—visions, angels, audible voices, promptings, etc.—we notice one very important and consistent fact. The extraordinary means of guidance were not sought. I don't deny that God can still speak to us in direct, surprising ways. Of course, it must always be tested against Scripture, but I believe God can still give visions. The point is that these extraordinary means in the New Testament are just that—extra-ordinary.

God may guide us in these ways in rare instances, but we should not expect Him to. We have no record in the New Testament of anyone anxious to hear God tell him what to do. Paul never sought out special words of knowledge concerning his future. He seems very concerned to know and obey God's moral will. But when he gets to a fork in the road, hesitating and pleading with God to know which way to go seems completely foreign to the apostle.

Longtime Old Testament scholar Bruce Waltke summarizes the biblical evidence well:

> Any time you take the Bible out of context you destroy the intent of God's Word. That's why you cannot take instances of special revelation and make them normative for the Christian experience. . . . When he [Paul] did experience a special revelation, seeing a vision of a man calling him to Macedonia, he obeyed. But the special revelation of God was a rare and unique experience, even for Paul. . . . We cannot take special circumstances and make them the norm by which we live our lives. Special revelation for guidance was not the normal apostolic experience. And at the time it was received (by Paul, by Philip, by Peter as he lay on his roof) it was not being sought. . . . Special revelation came at a time when God wanted to lead them apart from the normal ways in which His people make choices.[2]

We need to affirm, on the one hand, that God can still give visions or speak in extraordinary ways (though never in ways that add to or contradict the Scriptures). Even a conservative Reformed academic like Waltke says, "Too many conservative scholars have no place for God's special intercession because they have no control over it. We can't force God to talk, yet sometimes He completely surprises us and talks anyway."[3] But on the other hand, we must recognize that these ways are rare and not to be sought out as God's usual means of guiding His people.

WHAT ABOUT SPIRITUAL GIFTS?
THE ONGOING DEBATE

If you are familiar with the world of theological debates, you know that this matter of God's guidance touches on the question of spiritual gifts. On the one side are cessationists who believe that the "supernatural" gifts of the Spirit such as prophecy, tongues, and healing, ceased with the apostolic age (or perhaps later with the close of the biblical canon). On the other side are charismatics, or continuationists, who believe that all of the gifts of the Spirit are still operative in our day. Although there are serious differences between the two camps, representatives from both camps often land in almost identical places when it comes to God's guidance.

For example, in his excellent article, "Modern Spiritual Gifts as Analogous to Apostolic Gifts," Vern Poythress of Westminster Theological Seminary gives numerous historical examples from Reformers and Puritans who talked about strange impressions, or miraculous visions, or supernatural insight. They all assumed the end to some spiritual gifts, yet they did not immediately discount God's mysterious and surprising work. Poythress concludes:

> All of these extraordinary phenomena can be subsumed under the description in the Westminster Confession of Faith 5.3: "God, in his ordinary providence, maketh use of means, yet is free to work without, above, and against them, at his pleasure." God's works, so described, surely encompasses all nondiscursive [i.e., not learned through linear reasoning] processes. . . . But because of its strong commitment to the sovereignty of God and the mystery of his plan, the Confession acknowledges explicitly that there may also be operations that are not attached to means in any ordinary way. The ultimate determining factor in every case is "his pleasure."[4]

From the other side, Donald Gee of the charismatic Assemblies of God denomination warns:

> [There are] grave problems raised by the habit of giving and receiving personal "messages" of guidance through the gifts of the Spirit. . . . The Bible gives a place for such direction from the Holy Spirit. . . . But it must be kept in proportion. An examination of the Scriptures will show us that as a matter of fact the early Christians did not continually receive such voices from heaven. In most cases they made their decisions by the use of what we often call "sanctified common sense" and lived quite normal lives. Many of our errors where spiritual gifts are concerned arise when we want to make the extraordinary and exceptional to be made frequent

and habitual. Let all who develop excessive desire for "messages" through the gifts take warning from the wreckage of past generations as well as contemporaries. . . . The Holy Scriptures are a lamp unto our feet and a light unto our path.[5]

Many mature cessationists like Poythress who believe that certain gifts have ceased will also be quick to add, "But God surprises us nonetheless." And many mature charismatics like Gee who emphasize the continuing nature of all the gifts will also be quick to add, "But the Scriptures alone are our sure guide." There are still differences between the two positions, but both end up in similar places: God can use extraordinary means, but they are, by definition, out of the ordinary and not to be expected.

Why have this discussion in a book about God's will? Because I want to make sure with everything else I am saying in a book about seeking the will of God as revealed in Scripture for right decision making that you don't think I am suspicious every time someone claims to have heard from the Lord. Candidly, though, I'm just not blown away by these claims, either. If you think you've heard from God, I'm not ready to lock you up in the psych ward, nor am I ready to bless whatever you "heard" because you think God said it. Hearing from God directly can be important and legitimate, but I certainly wouldn't treat a special impression from the Lord as more special than the sure word of the Lord found in the Bible.

7

TOOLS
of the
TRADE

I wonder if you saw this report in the news a few years ago:

MAN, 91, DIES WAITING FOR WILL OF GOD

Tupelo, Miss.—Walter Houston, described by family members as a devoted Christian, died Monday after waiting seventy years for God to give him clear direction about what to do with his life.

"He hung around the house and prayed a lot, but just never got that confirmation," his wife Ruby says. "Sometimes he thought he heard God's voice, but then he wouldn't be sure, and he'd start the process all over again."

Houston, she says, never really figured out what his life was about, but felt content to pray continuously about what he might do for the Lord. Whenever he was about to take action, he would pull back, "because he didn't want to disappoint God or go against him in any way," Ruby says. "He was very sensitive to always remaining in God's will. That was primary to him."

Friends say they liked Walter, though he seemed not to capitalize on his talents.

"Walter had a number of skills he never got around to using," says longtime friend Timothy Burns. "He worked very well with wood and had a storyteller side to him too. I always told him, 'Take a risk. Try something new if you're not happy,' but he was too afraid of letting the Lord down."

To his credit, they say, Houston, who worked mostly as a handyman, was able to pay off the mortgage on the couple's modest home.

If you saw this report, then you must be a fan of larknews. com, which has a "funny because it could be true" collection of fake Christian news.[1] The story about Walter Houston is not real. But it is almost believable, isn't it? At the rate some of us are going, we will be exploring our future career at thirty, entering adulthood at forty, trying to find ourselves at fifty, questioning everything again at sixty, pondering a career move at seventy, wondering what we were made for at eighty, and still waiting to discover God's will at ninety.

And then we'll die, never having done much of anything. If we had done something—almost anything, really—faithfully and humbly and for God's glory for all that time, we could have made quite an impact. But if we do nothing, because we are always trying to figure out the perfect something, when it comes time to show what we did for the Lord, we will not have anything.

Over the years, anxious, risk-averse Christians have developed a number of tools for discerning God's will. In this chapter, I'll mention four of these tools of the trade: open doors, fleeces, random Bible verses, and impressions. All four tools can be used wisely. And all four can be instruments of foolishness.

OPEN DOORS
(AND DON'T BE AFRAID TO KNOCK)

Christians often speak of "an open door" from the Lord, meaning, "God is giving me this great opportunity." Conversely, when things don't seem to be going our way, we talk of God "closing a door," or removing some possible opportunity.

This sort of thinking can be good if we see the open door as an opportunity to do something we already know is good, like sharing the gospel with a neighbor or taking a job to feed your family even though it's not the work you've always wanted. Likewise, if "an open door" simply means "there's one more spot in the study-abroad program and I think I'll take it," that's fine too. In such cases, when we speak of open doors, we are merely referring to opportunities God has given us to do the good things we already wanted to do.

But there are foolish ways to use this "open door" theology. Christians are sometimes guilty of using the absence of an open door as an excuse for laziness: "I put my resumé on Monster. com last week and no one has contacted me. The Lord just isn't opening any doors." Perhaps, but maybe you should make some phone calls, knock on some doors, and visit every potential employer in town before you blame your unemployment on God.

Likewise, Christians often use "open door" theology to bless whatever bad idea they've already decided to do: "I know my marriage is in shambles, and my wife wants me around more so we can work things out, but God has opened a door for me to get a big promotion. The work will require me to travel thirty weeks a year and be away from my wife more than ever, but God must be leading me to take this job or else He wouldn't have opened this door."

Similarly, we sometimes take the easy way out and then spiritualize our cowardice by claiming, "It was an open door." For example, don't think to yourself, *I need to call and have a difficult conversation with my sister. I should really talk with her, but my cell phone is out of minutes, so the Lord must want me to send an e-mail instead.* Don't think the convenient way is always God's way of making a more comfortable way for you. Was an available ship sailing to Tarshish the Lord's open door for Jonah? Was this a "favorable providence" confirming that Jonah's decision to turn away from Nineveh was the right one? Of course not. The next ship to Tarshish had nothing to do with the Lord's leading and everything to do with Jonah's disobedience.[2]

Here's the bottom line: If God opens the door for you to do something you know is good or necessary, be thankful for the opportunity. But other than that, don't assume that the relative ease or difficulty of a new situation is God's way of telling you to do one thing or the other. Remember, God's will for your life is your sanctification, and God tends to use discomfort and trials more than comfort and ease to make us holy.

FLEE THE FLEECE!

What Christian, in the midst of a perplexing quandary, hasn't been inspired by Gideon to lay out a metaphorical fleece before God?[3] I recall one time when I was young, facing some inconsequential decision, no doubt, when I actually set a shirt out on the floor and was ready to call on the Lord for dew. But I couldn't decide if I wanted the Lord to make the shirt wet or keep it dry. I knew that if I wanted to be confirmed in my decision, I should probably ask the Lord to keep the shirt dry (since the normal dew fall in my bedroom was pretty minimal). But that didn't seem very suspenseful. So I pondered asking for a wet shirt in the morning. But was I really going to base my decision on whether God would hearken to my call for a moistened miracle? I was confused. In the end, I gave up on the fleece idea and went to sleep.

Although making decisions by testing God with fleeces is generally a bad idea, sometimes it can look similar to setting reasonable goals. For example, suppose you are considering running a marathon. But you decide that you won't sign up for the 26.2 mile race unless you first lose fifteen pounds and finish a half-marathon. In a way this sounds like laying out a fleece, but it is really just prudence and good goal setting.

Humble goals and loosely held plans are good. Expecting God to do tricks for us is bad. Don't pray: "God, if You want me to go out on this date, then make my professors cancel all their assignments for the weekend. If You don't do that, I'll just tell Josh that it wasn't the Lord's will that we go out." The whole fleece approach to life is dangerously close to violating Jesus' admonition, "You shall not put the Lord your God to the test" (Matthew 4:7).

Now, I know Gideon asked God for some special dew. But there are good reasons to think Gideon's request is not a normative example. For starters, Gideon didn't have a Bible. More than likely, he didn't have a single page of God's inspired Word of his own. More importantly, the book of Judges generally does not provide a good example of much of anything. When the theme of the book is "everyone did what was right in his own eyes" (Judges 21:25), we should think twice before copying whatever practices or attitudes we find in its chapters. Gideon's request was probably an indication of cowardice and unbelief more than faithful, wise decision making.

RANDOM IS AS RANDOM DOES

Sadly, some Christians put greater stock in the Word of God when it is randomly selected than when it is read chapter by chapter, day after day. The Bible carries no greater weight just because verses are flipped to at random.

Having said that, however, we can be thankful for the times God speaks to us in the Scriptures in a poignant way and tells us just what we need to hear. Suppose you have been struggling with pornography again. You feel very distant from God and you haven't read your Bible in weeks. But you feel a nudge to read it this morning. So you pick up your Bible and, not knowing where to start, decide to read the Sermon on the Mount. Very quickly you get to Matthew 5:8, "Blessed are the pure in heart for they shall see God." You are struck to the core, absolutely convicted of your impurity and the vision of God you are missing as a result.

Now did God want you to read that verse at that moment? Sure. God could have used a thousand other verses to speak to you, but He used that one for you in a specific way. God does that sort of thing all the time. He brings verses to mind. He gives us a powerful sermon in our moment of great need. He leads us to a passage of Scripture that says just what He wants to say.

So the problem is not with God's mysterious ability to direct us to the right verses. The problem is not only in treating random verses as holier than other kinds of Bible reading, but in taking verses out of context and making them say things they were never meant to say. I can imagine a young man dating a girl named Becky. He is considering marriage, but he's not sure. So he asks the Lord to give him a sign. Well, the day is January 24 and his Bible reading plan has him reading from Genesis 24 (NIV). He gets to the end of the chapter and reads "and he married Rebekah. So she became his wife, and he loved her." The young man takes it as a sure word from the Lord to propose to Becky. To delay any longer would be disobedience. Or what about the woman who turns at random to 2 Samuel 7:3: "Go, do all that is in your heart, for the

Lord is with you"? Is that always good advice, straight from the Lord?

Maybe you've heard the joke about the man who was hoping to get a word from the Lord and happened to turn to Matthew 27:5 where it says that Judas "went and hanged himself." Not happy with this word for the day, the man flipped his Bible open to another page, where his eyes descended upon Luke 10:37, "And Jesus said to him, 'You go, and do likewise.'"

> John Newton was wise enough to see the folly in seeking guidance through random Bible verses.

These may be extreme examples, but they are not too far removed from how many Christians approach the Bible. Even if the answers seem thrilling in their relevance, we must not put any stock in anachronistic, out-of-context answers we read into the Bible after asking questions the Bible never intended to address.

The great hymn writer and pastor John Newton (1725–1807) knew this truth. Once he was considering a call to a church in Warwick, England. At first, Newton thought God was promising him great success if he took the call. "I remember, in going to undertake the care of a congregation, I was reading, as I walked in the green lane, 'Fear not, Paul, I have much people in this city.' But I soon afterward was disappointed to find that Paul was not John and that Corinth was not Warwick."[4] Newton realized that while the Bible may promise many things, it did not promise him great success in Warwick. He was wise enough to see the folly in seeking guidance through random Bible verses.

"Others, when in doubt, have opened the Bible at a venture," Newton wrote elsewhere, "and expected to find something to direct them in the first verse they should cast their eye upon. It is no small discredit to this practice that the heathens, who knew not the Bible, used some of their favorite books in the same way . . . for if people will be governed by the occurrence of a single text of Scripture, without regarding the context, or duly comparing it with the general tenor of the word of God, and with their own circumstances, they may commit the greatest extravagances, expect the greatest impossibilities, and contradict the plainest dictates of common sense, while they think they have the word of God on their side."[5]

IMPRESSIONS AS IMPRESSION

We all go with our gut at times. That is to say, we make decisions based on a feeling or our intuition. We get an impression of what to do and we do it. Quite often there is nothing wrong with this approach. It may even be very good if the nudge we feel is to do something we already know is good, like give a cup of cold water to a stranger in need. This book is not designed to make us all into hyper-rationalistic decision-makers who need to consult an Excel spreadsheet before deciding on an appetizer from Applebees. The last thing I want is to keep everyone from acting on subjectivity or unexplained impressions.

This book is called *Just Do Something,* after all, not *Just Do Nothing Until You Are Positive You Aren't Making a Mistake.*

> Don't confuse hunches and subjective feelings with certain words from the Lord.

So the problem with impressions is not that they are subjective. The problem is in assuming they are from the Lord. Here's my profound wisdom on the matter: Impressions are impressions. They are not in a special category. Don't confuse impressions, hunches, and subjective feelings with certain words from the Lord. If a thought or impulse pops into your head, even if it happens while reading Scripture, don't assume it is a voice from heaven.

We all get intuitions and hunches and gut feelings all the time. Some are from the Lord. Some aren't. Most often, it probably doesn't matter. Listen to your gut or not, but don't make it an extra-special factor in your decision making, and don't think you need that peaceful, easy feeling before you can make up your mind.

On a related note, we need to be careful that we don't absolutize our decisions just because we pray about them. Church boards or denominational committees are often guilty of putting their decisions out of reach because "the matter was bathed in prayer." Certainly prayer makes a huge difference. I am more apt to listen to others or be listened to if there has been a season of earnest prayer. But impressions of the Lord's leading after prayer are still impressions. We cannot infallibly judge the rightness or wrongness of our plans based on the feelings we have about them after prayer. We may feel anxious, even after prayer, about a hard task we really should not avoid. Conversely, we can also deceive ourselves, wanting something so badly that we imagine the Lord is answering us according to our wishes. That's why I will not put God's infallible seal of approval on the plans of our church board just because we prayed about them. I will encourage the church to trust their leaders, and assure them that we asked for wisdom and prayed to be submissive to the Lord, but on issues not clearly laid out in Scripture, I don't want to claim more authority for our plans than the nature of impressions allows.

DON'T MANIPULATE OR ABUSE
THE TOOLS OF THE TRADE

Open doors, fleeces, random Bible verses, and impressions, if construed in the right way, have their place in the Christian's life. But in my experience, these tools have been wielded for more harm than good. They are easily abused, manipulated, and lend themselves to superstition.

A far better approach is once again laid out by John Newton: "In general, he [God] guides and directs his people by affording them, in answer to prayer, the light of his Holy Spirit, which enables them to understand and to love the Scriptures. The Word of God is not to be used as a lottery; nor is it designed to instruct us by shreds and scraps, which, detached from their proper places, have no determinative import; but it is to furnish us with just principles, right apprehensions to regulate our judgments and affections, and thereby to influence and direct our conduct."[6]

There's a word for this approach to guidance and the will of God—wisdom. It's not sexy, and it requires no secret decoder ring. But it is the way to "understand righteousness and justice and equity, every good path" (Proverbs 2:9).

8

The WAY of WISDOM

They say we live in the information age, with more books, radio stations, satellite/cable TV channels, and talking heads than ever. And when you add the Internet to the mix, we have billions of pieces of information at our fingertips.

But wisdom is harder to find than information. A while back I was trying to figure something out about the Peloponnesian War between Athens and Sparta, so I Googled it and got 614,000 hits. For fun, I tried *salamanders* and got 1,600,000. Even cooler, *Mr. T.* of Mohawk haircut and "I pity the fool" TV fame netted 6,300,000 results. Judging by the Internet, B. A. Baracus, Mr. T's rough-and-tumble character on *The A-Team*, has been more critical to civilization than anything Thucydides ever wrote about. We have more information than ever before, and yet our wisdom has not kept pace with our knowledge. In fact, you could make a good case that where information has increased, wisdom has decreased.

Take the news, for example. We watch twenty-four-hour news channels so, we imagine, we will be informed about the crucial events shaping our world. But all we really know is what people are talking about right now, most of which will prove monumentally insignificant in a month.[1] And even when we do get helpful information, it's surrounded by so much unhelpful information that it's hard to put things in perspective.

These were the headlines on CNN.com on a Tuesday afternoon back in 2007: "Bush to call for sharp cutback in gas consumption." "Military: 4 held in sneak attack on U.S. in Iraq." "Libby: White House wanted to sacrifice me for Rove." "Smoking gun report to say global warming is here." "Shark chomps head of man diving for weeds." "Oscar nominations announced." "Sex offender, 29, enrolled himself in seventh grade." "Sea lion misses water, ends up on dairy farm." "101 dumbest moments in business." "Tulsa digging up car buried 50 years."

These are the *top* stories, mind you. Do you remember any of these two years later? Or even two days later? How much of it actually matters? And if something really did matter in this list, how could you recognize it when it is surrounded by breaking news about the daily travails of sea lions? We have plenty of information. Not enough wisdom.

TAKE THE GOD-CENTERED APPROACH

Wisdom is what we need to live a godly life. God does not tell us the future, nor does He expect us to figure it out. When we don't know which way to turn and are faced with tough decisions in life, God doesn't expect us to grope in the dark for some hidden will of direction. He expects us to trust Him and to be wise. This is the theme of Proverbs, especially chapter 2. Consider verses 1–6 (NIV):

> *My son, if you accept my words and store up my commands within you, turning your ear to wisdom and applying your heart to understanding, and if you call out for insight and cry aloud for understanding, and if you look for it as for silver and search for it as for hidden treasure, then you will understand the fear of the Lord and find the knowledge of God. For the Lord gives wisdom, and from his mouth come knowledge and understanding.*

Verse 5 gives the answer to the question, "What is wisdom?" Wisdom is understanding the fear of the Lord and finding the knowledge of God. Wisdom, in Proverbs, is always moral. The fool, the opposite of the wise person, is not a moron or an oaf. The fool is the person who does not live life God's way. Wisdom is knowing God and doing as He commands. Foolishness, on the other hand, is turning from God and listening only to yourself. So when we talk about wisdom, we are talking about more than witty aphorisms and homespun advice. We are talking about a profoundly God-centered approach to life. Biblical wisdom means living a disciplined and prudent life in the fear of the Lord.

Proverbs 2 not only tells us what wisdom is but what our attitude should be toward wisdom. Our attitude should be one of earnest longing. Wisdom, for the Christian, is more precious than silver or gold.

> Our attitude toward wisdom should be one of earnest longing.

Imagine if someone came to you tonight and said, "I'll pay off all your bills. I'll pay off your mortgage. I'll load up your Roth IRA. I'll give you money for vacations. I'll give you 20,000 square feet to live in, and any car you like, *or* I can make you wise." What would you say to that person? If you fear the Lord, you'll take wisdom in a heartbeat.

Isn't it interesting that we are never told in Scripture to ask God to reveal the future or to show us His plan for our lives? But we are told—in no uncertain terms—to call out for insight and to cry aloud for understanding. In other words, God says, "Don't ask to see all the plans I've made for you. Ask Me for wisdom so you'll know how to live according to My Book."

Wisdom is precious because it keeps us from foolishness. If you turn to Proverbs 2, you'll notice the "if-then" construction of this chapter: If you do this, you get wisdom. Specifically, *if* you accept my words (v. 2), and *if* you call out for insight (3), and *if* you look for wisdom as for silver (4), *then* you will understand the fear of the Lord (5), and *then* you will understand what is right and just and fair (9). Verses 5–11 show you everything you have when you get wisdom. You have understanding and knowledge (5–6) and protection (8) and a good path (9).

Just as important, having wisdom keeps you from real dangers. Verses 12–22 show you that wisdom keeps you from wicked men (12), dark ways (13), crooked paths (15), and the adulterous woman with her seductive speech (16). Wisdom is the path of righteousness (20), while foolishness is the path of death (18–19).

So how do we get this valuable wisdom? Our text mentions three ways. The first way to get wisdom is to store up God's commands (1). The second way is turn your ear to wisdom (2). And the third way is to call out for insight (3). To put these ways into familiar language, we could say we get wisdom by reading our Bibles (storing up God's commands), listening to sound advice (turning our ears to wisdom), and praying to God (calling out for insight). The second and third are nearly interchangeable because when God gives us wisdom, He most often gives it through other people. But for the sake of organization we'll look at them as distinct.

WALKING THE WAY OF WISDOM: SCRIPTURE

God's Word is living and active. When we read the Bible, we hear from God with a confidence we find in no other book and from no other voice. We can read the Scriptures knowing that this is what the Holy Spirit says. And as we read and reread and ponder and study and digest the Scriptures, we will, as 2 Timothy 3:15 says, become "wise for salvation."

But the Bible is not a casebook. It doesn't give us explicit information about dating or careers or when to build a church or buy a house. We've all wished that the Bible was that kind of book, but it's not because God is interested in more than getting us to follow His to-do list; He wants transformation. God doesn't want us to merely give external obedience to His commands. He wants us to know Him so intimately that His thoughts become our thoughts, His ways our ways, His affections our affections. God wants us to drink so deeply of the Scriptures that our heads and hearts are transformed so that we love what He loves and hate what He hates.

Romans 12:1–2 is the classic text about this kind of spiritual transformation.

> *I appeal to you therefore, brothers, by the mercies of God, to present your bodies as a living sacrifice, holy and acceptable to God, which is your spiritual worship. Do not be conformed to this world, but be transformed by the renewal of your mind, that by testing you may discern what is the will of God, what is good and acceptable and perfect.*

There are three commands here: (1) Present your bodies as living sacrifices. (2) Do not conform to the world. (3) Be transformed by the renewal of your mind. If we do these three things, then we will be able to discern what God's will is. This is how the Christian life works. There are no shortcuts. We don't get secret messages that tell us whether to drop the entomology minor. God wants us to offer ourselves to Him, turn from the ways of the world, and be transformed. Then we will have something better than special revelations and words about the future—we'll have wisdom.

God wants us to develop a taste for godliness. My wife, Trisha, really doesn't appreciate that I have—how shall I put it?—a sensitive palate. To put it less charitably, I am a very picky eater. There are lots of foods I

> **Eat, swallow, and digest the Word of God.**

don't like (too many), and I can often detect new ingredients in a familiar recipe. My lovely wife generally isn't thrilled to hear my exceptional discoveries: "This looks like strawberry-banana Jell-O, but I think I taste some strawberry-kiwi in here," for example. I am a lifelong Jell-O eater—several bowls almost every Sunday growing up. So I've developed a taste for Jell-O—with or without Cool Whip and with or without ice cream. (Yes, you can and should put ice cream in Jell-O.) I know Jell-O brand versus off-brand. But it's taken a lifetime of Jell-O eating to acquire this exquisite taste. (I can also tell when my wife skimps on the butter with the macaroni and cheese and when she puts wheat germ in the chocolate chip cookies, but I'll save that for marriage counseling.)

That's how we are to be with the Word of God. We must eat it and swallow it and digest it so regularly that over time we develop a taste for godliness. That's wisdom.

Wisdom is the difference between knowing a world-class biologist who can write your papers for you and studying under a world-class biologist so that you can write the kind of papers he would write. Too many of us want God to be the world-class scholar who will write our papers and live our lives for us, when God wants us to sit at His feet and read His Word so that we can live a life in the image of His Son. God doesn't tell us the future for this simple, yet profound reason: We become what we behold. God wants us to behold Him in His glory so that we can be transformed into His likeness (2 Corinthians 3:18). If God figured everything out for us, we wouldn't need to focus on Him and learn to delight in His glory. God says, "I'm not giving you a crystal ball. I'm giving you My Word. Meditate on it; see Me in it; and become like Me."

WALKING THE WAY OF WISDOM: COUNSEL

Those who are wise read and memorize Scripture. They love to hear it read, preached, and sung. But the wise also know you need to read the Bible in community. You need to listen to what other Bible-reading Christians say. If we want to make wise decisions, we must seek advice and counsel from others. This is especially true when dealing with nonethical choices or decisions that aren't clearly laid out in Scripture. It's not that we always listen to the majority in everything, or that the decisions we make will always please everyone, or that every friend in your circle must be consulted before making a decision. But when God's Word doesn't speak decisively, or when the matter facing us isn't even considered in Scripture, it is wise to listen to other Christians.

Consider these words from Proverbs:

> *Let the wise hear and increase in learning, and the one who un-*
> *derstands obtain guidance.*(1:5)
> *The way of a fool is right in his own eyes, but a wise man listens*
> *to advice.* (12:15)
> *Without counsel plans fail, but with many advisers they succeed.*
> (15:22)
> *Listen to advice and accept instruction, that you may gain wis-*
> *dom in the future.* (19:20)

One of the virtues I appreciate most in others, and it's a virtue I hope I have in some measure, is teachability. Are you willing to change your mind when another person's case has more merit than yours? Are you able to hear good advice when it comes from some mouth other than your own and may even contradict your preconceived ideas? Are you willing to admit "I didn't think of that" or "I see your point"? If no one has ever heard you change your mind about something, then you are either a god or you have mistaken yourself for one. I can say without a doubt that I make better decisions when I consult with my wife. I make better decisions with the elders rather than without them. I am wiser when I listen to my friends first.

Now, of course, often you just have to decide things on your own. And sometimes you need to make an unpopular decision because you know it's right. But for most of our decisions we would do well to simply ask someone else, "What do you think?" We spend all this time asking God, "What's Your will?" when He's probably thinking, "Make a friend, would you? Go talk to someone. There's a reason I've redeemed a lot of you—because you do fewer dumb things when you talk to each other. Get some advice. You might just hear My voice."

WALKING THE WAY OF WISDOM: PRAYER

The way of wisdom means three things: searching the Scriptures, seeking wise counsel, and praying to God. But what do we pray for if we aren't asking God to tell us exactly what to do? Well, first of all we pray for illumination. We ask God to open our minds so we can understand the Scriptures and apply them to our lives. Don't forget about this prayer. God can show you amazingly relevant things in His Word if you ask Him to. Second, pray for wisdom. We have not because we ask not. God *wants* us to make good decisions that will help us be more like Christ and bring Him glory. Third, pray for things that you already know are God's will. Pray for good motives in your decision making. Pray for an attitude of trust and faith and obedience. Pray for humility and teachability. Pray for His gospel to spread. You know that He wants these things in the world and for your life. Pray for them. Seek first His kingdom and His righteousness, as Jesus asked us to (Matthew 6:33).

> The way of wisdom is a way of life. And that makes you freer than you realize.

And then after you've prayed and studied and sought

advice, make a decision and don't hyper-spiritualize it. Do what seems best. Sometimes you won't have time to pray and read and seek counsel for a month. That's why the way of wisdom is about more than getting a decisive word about one or two big decisions in life. The way of wisdom is a way of life. And when it's a way of life, you are freer than you realize. If you are drinking deeply of godliness in the Word and from others and in your prayer life, then you'll probably make God-honoring decisions. In fact, if you are a person of prayer, full of regular good counsel from others, and steeped in the truth of the Word, you should begin to make many important decisions instinctively, and some of them even quickly. For most Christians, agonizing over decisions is the only sure thing we know to do, the only thing that feels safe and truly spiritual. But sometimes, oftentimes actually, it's okay to just decide.

A while back I was on the phone with a nice Christian man asking me if I would be willing to do a small speaking gig sometime in the following year. I got some more information over the phone and checked out the dates as we were talking. Everything seemed to work. I would be away less than twenty-four hours, and I could speak on something I already had basically prepared. I told him that I would be willing to come. He told me I could have time to pray about it. I noted again that the dates worked, it was still a long way off (so I could plan accordingly), the subject was fine, and I'd be happy to do it. But my yes didn't stick. He politely insisted that I should pray about it. So I prayed about it and called back the next day saying yes again.

Now, the last thing I want to do is discourage people from praying. After all, prayer is the third key in seeking wisdom. But isn't it possible that if we are walking with God in daily prayer, and we have some sanctified common sense, that we should be able to make decisions on the spot once in a while? Certainly we have been spared poor decisions by waiting and thinking, but we can also miss good opportunities and waste valuable time by grinding the wheels of choice into a pseudo-spiritual halt before we pencil something in on the Day-Timer.

Study the Scriptures, listen to others, and pray continually —that's the best course of action, not just at the moment of crisis, but as a way of life. And as you engage in these practices, don't forget to make a decision—always with wisdom, always with freedom, and sometimes even with speed.

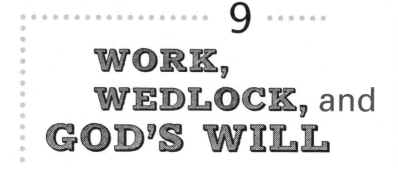

9

WORK, WEDLOCK, and GOD'S WILL

Wisdom sounds good, but how does it work? If the way of wisdom involves searching the Scriptures, getting wise counsel, praying, and finally making a decision, how do we walk in this way when it comes to life's tough decisions? In this chapter, we'll look at two choices that tend to throw sensitive Christians into a tizzy of self-reflection and pietistic passivity: work and marriage.

GET A JOB

Let's start with the job question. Whether you're facing a choice between two jobs or considering a career change or just beginning to explore your vocational possibilities, how does godly wisdom help you make a decision?

Step One: Search the Scriptures. Remember, you're not looking for a verse that says, "Take thou the cashier position at the Piggly Wiggly." You are looking for principles. So for starters you want to know whether the job is righteous. Assuming you're not considering a gig as a hit man for the mob or a photographer (or model!) for *Playboy*, most jobs can be God-glorifying (but not all are, so do ask this question).

Besides searching the Scriptures to see if the job itself is okay, you want to be thinking about other biblical principles.

> A good Bible-preaching, caring church nearby should be a top factor in your decision.

The Scripture warns us, "If anyone does not provide for his relatives, and especially for members of his household, he has denied the faith and is worse than an unbeliever" (1 Timothy 5:8). Some jobs may put your family at risk of discomfort or limited possessions (like missionaries, for example), and that's not always bad. But you do need to be able to provide for your family.

You also want to consider the churches available where you are taking a job. Sadly, this is a part of obeying the Scriptures that most Christians rarely consider. Before taking a new job, we look at salary, benefits, school districts, commuting time, and cultural amenities; but if everything else falls into place and there's no good church in the area, it's hard to imagine how God's revealed will—your sanctification—will be well-served. Obviously, you may intentionally take a job somewhere where there aren't churches in hopes that you can evangelize and maybe even start a church. But for most of the people who will move somewhere else in the United States or Canada, whether or not there is a good Bible-believing, Bible-preaching, caring church nearby should be a top factor in your decision.

Don't think only about safety or the resale value of your house or the school system. Think about what ministry you can do and what church you can be a part of and whether you can get there in a reasonable car drive. The more you read the Bible, the more your thinking will be transformed, and the more these kinds of issues will matter to you.

Step Two: Get wise counsel. Talk to people who know you well. What skills and abilities do they see in you? Do you like kids and have fun with them? If not, you probably shouldn't be a kindergarten teacher. Ask your friends what your gifts are. Ask them, "Can you see me doing this?" Listen to your friends, your parents, your teachers, your leaders. Be teachable. It may be that you're not very responsible and you're not hardworking and someone will tell you that. Or it may be that you're looking for work you're completely unqualified for. Maybe you don't have the proper training, or maybe you need work that offers frequent change, or something with more structure. If a couple of friends suggest you aren't very natural with people, selling vacuum cleaners door-to-door probably is a bad fit. In any event, get good advice and be willing to listen.

Step Three: Pray. Let me give an example that may give you some ideas of what to pray for when considering a job change. I mentioned earlier the decision I faced as to whether to come to University Reformed Church or stay at the church in Iowa where I was quite content. I prayed a lot about the decision. But I didn't ask God to tell me what to do. So what did I pray for? I prayed that God would make me honest in my interviews. I prayed that I would see a true picture of this church and that they would see a true picture of me. I prayed mostly that my heart would be right, that I wouldn't be motivated by pride—either to stay because it was a big church or to move because I could be the senior pastor. I prayed that I wouldn't make a decision based on fear: "What if I fail as a senior pastor?" "What if everyone in Iowa gets mad at me for going?" Or pleasing people: "I don't want to let down the search committee that's been working at this for so long."

I prayed that I would make a decision based on faith, hope, and love—and not the praise of man and greed and selfish ambition. In other words, I prayed that I would be following God's will of desire rather than praying to figure out His will of direction.

Step Four: Make a decision. Don't over-spiritualize. You can serve the Lord in a thousand different jobs. We need missionaries and we need pastors. But we also need entrepreneurs who create jobs so people can make money so they can support missionaries and pastors. And we need entrepreneurs because work is good. Please don't ever think you are a second-class citizen in the kingdom of God if you aren't in full-time ministry. You can honor the Lord as a teacher, mother, doctor, lawyer, loan officer, or social worker; you can work in retail, fast food, politics, or big business; you can be a butcher, a baker, or a candlestick maker. You can be just about anything you want as long as you aren't lazy (Proverb 6:6–11; 26:13–16), and whatever you do you perform to the glory of God (1 Corinthians 10:31).

God calls His people to lots of different things. Sometimes you feel a sense of calling to your job and, you know what, sometimes you don't. You just work. I'm extremely thankful that I love what I do for a living. I feel badly for people who only tolerate their jobs, or worse. But we must all serve the Lord with heart, soul, strength, and mind wherever He's placed us. Unfortunately, we've turned the idea of calling or vocation on its head. The Reformers emphasized calling in order to break down the sacred-secular divide. They said, if you are working for the glory of God, you are doing the Lord's work, no matter whether you're a priest or a monk or a banker. But we've taken this notion of calling and turned it upside down, so instead of finding purpose in every kind of work, we are madly looking for the one job that will fulfill our purpose in life.

> Contentment says, "God has me here for a reason, and if He never does anything different, I'll still serve and praise Him."

I'm not arguing for complacency in or bitter resignation to your present circumstances. I am arguing for what the apostle Paul advocated: godliness with contentment. The two together form "great gain," he declared (1 Timothy 6:6). Complacency and contentment are often confused, but there is a difference between the two. Contentment is saying, "God has me here for a reason, and if He never does anything different, I'll still serve and praise Him." Complacency is saying, "Things will never change, so why bother trying?" The complacent are like wine left with the dregs, like coffee sludge at the bottom of your cup, like the wicked "who say in their hearts, 'The Lord will not do good, nor will he do ill' " (Zephaniah 1:12). Nothing is impossible with God, so go ahead and run hard after your big plans and take a shot at your dream job. But remember that in almost any job, God can be pleased with your work so long as you are taking pleasure in Him as you do it.

GETTING HITCHED

It seems that getting married is getting harder to do, or at least harder to commit to. In 1965, the median age at first marriage was 22.8 for men and 20.6 for women. By 2002, a little more than a generation later, the median age for marriage rose to 26.9 for men and 25.3 for women.[1] Delayed marriage occurs for numerous reasons: longer life spans, the drive for more education, transient lifestyles among the young, greater discretionary income, a desire for more experiences before marriage, and greater (and habitual) independence. Add to these the opportunities to meet hundreds of potential mates, leading to more second-guessing and indecision.

For Christians there is another delaying factor: searching for the will of God in marriage. *What decision,* we think to ourselves, *is more important than picking a husband or wife? Surely, God wants to, in fact,* must *tell me who is the right guy for me.*

Such an approach sounds spiritual, but wisdom points us in a different direction. The four steps we applied to the job search can also be used in the pursuit of marriage. (That's the thing about wisdom; it's less of a detailed road map and more of a way to make decisions in many different situations.)

Step One: Search the Scriptures. The Bible won't tell you whom to marry, but it does tell you something about marriage. Marriage should be between one man and one woman. Christians should marry Christians (cf. Malachi 2:11; 1 Corinthians 7:39). We should not be unequally yoked (2 Corinthians 6:14). I wouldn't advise a very mature believer to marry someone who converted yesterday, nor would I recommend a Protestant marry a Catholic, nor an evangelical wed a more liberal Christian. Those marriages still work out sometimes, but that's not the model. You want to yoke yourself to someone who is going to be plowing in the same direction you are.

Christians should also be circumspect before marrying someone who has been divorced. If the divorce did not take place on biblical grounds (e.g., sexual immorality [Matthew 19:9] or desertion by an unbelieving spouse [1 Corinthians 7:15]), then Jesus says you are committing adultery because you are marrying someone who should still be married to his or her spouse (Matthew 5:31–32).

Step Two: Get wise counsel. Do your friends think this marriage makes sense? Do they see you growing and flourishing when you're around him, or do they sense that you get moody and frustrated whenever you are together? Even more importantly, what do your parents think? It's true that sometimes parents object to marriages for all the wrong reasons. But in this country we probably honor our parents less than we should and are too impatient with them and try too little to bring them along and hear them out when they aren't excited about a boyfriend or girlfriend.

Step Three: Pray. Ask God for pure motives. You don't want to get married for lust or money or for fear of being single. You certainly don't want to get married to spite an ex-girlfriend or show an ex-boyfriend that you are desirable after all. Ask God that He would help you be honest about who you are and that you might know the other person for who she really is. Ask God for help not to make a decision based on your hormones, and that you won't refuse to make a decision out of cowardice.

Finally, pray less that God would show you who is the right husband or wife and pray more to *be* the right kind of husband or wife. If everyone was praying to be the right spouse, it wouldn't matter nearly so much who is the "right" spouse. Dump your list of the seventeen things you need in a wife and make yourself a list of seventeen things you need to be as a husband.

Step Four: Make a decision. I know this may sound crass, and your parents might not appreciate the advice, but guys, if you like a girl and you're both Christians and your friends and family aren't alarmed and she actually likes you back, you should probably get married. Let me be quick to add that singleness is not a disease in need of a cure. God can lead you into a time (or lifetime) of fruitful ministry as a single person. And if you at times feel frustration over an earnest longing to be married, remember this time of being single is part of God's good plan too. The church, for her part, needs to do a better job reaching out to singles, not treating them like misfits or as simply married people waiting to happen.

So I want to be clear: There's nothing wrong with being single. But gentlemen, there is something wrong with waiting around for God to pluck a woman from your side. He did it for Adam, but He's not going to do it for you. No matter who you marry, it will be hard work. So find someone to marry and work at it. You may get cold feet before walking down the aisle—that's normal. But don't overthink yourself into lifelong celibacy.

Too many young guys are waiting for writing in the sky before they make a relational commitment. It doesn't have to be that complicated. My grandpa DeYoung met my grandma on his paper route.

> Gentlemen . . . be the relational and spiritual leader God has called you to be.

Then they worked at the bowling alley together and started hanging out at the soda fountain. Eventually my grandpa proposed and they got married in 1948. When I asked him if he agonized over the decision to get married, he paused for a moment and said, "Uh . . . no. Was I supposed to?"

Gentlemen, there are wonderful Christian girls waiting for you to act, well, like a man. Stop waiting for romantic lightning to strike. Stop waiting for the umpteenth green light. Stop "hanging out" every night without ever making your intentions clear. Go ask a girl on a date, or ask her "to court," or whatever you think is the appropriate language. But do something. If you want to be single, that's great. Jesus was single. I hear it can be a pretty good gig. But if you want to get married, do something about it. Take a chance. Risk rejection. Be the relational and spiritual leader God has called you to be.

There are always plenty of exceptions, but as a general rule, Christians are waiting too long to get married. There are too many great Christians out there who should be married to one of the other great Christians out there. I remember Elisabeth Elliot saying one time that while speaking at a large Christian singles ministry, she desperately wanted to line up all the men on one wall, all the women on the other, count off (1, 1; 2, 2; 3, 3) and pair up those singles, and get them married.

Let me say it one more time: There is nothing wrong with being single. It can be a gift from the Lord and a gift to the church. But when there is an overabundance of Christian singles who want to be married, this is a problem. And it's a problem I put squarely at the feet of young men whose immaturity, passivity, and indecision are pushing their hormones to the limits of self-control, delaying the growing-up process, and forcing countless numbers of young women to spend lots of time and money pursuing a career (which is not necessarily wrong) when they would rather be getting married and having children. Men, if you want to be married, find a godly gal, treat her right, talk to her parents, pop the question, tie the knot, and start making babies.

IS THIS THE ONE?

And while I'm jumping on toes, let me explode the myth of "the one." Yes, in God's secret providence, He has just the right person picked out for you. And yes, once you meet the guy of your dreams, you won't want to be with anyone else. He'll be the only one for you. I know this will sound very un-romantic (especially to some of the ladies), but don't think that there is only one person on the whole planet to whom you could be happily married. You're not looking for that one puzzle piece that will interlock with yours. "You complete me" may sound magically romantic, but it's not true. Yes, men and women are designed to rely on one another in marriage. However, the biblical formula for marriage is not half a person plus half a person equals one completed puzzle of a person. Genesis math says one plus one equals one (Genesis 2:24).

I'm not saying you shouldn't "fit" with your spouse. And, of course, once you're married he or she will be the only puzzle piece for you. But before that don't think that *I've met this great gal, but what if she's not the one? What if the one is in Boise and I haven't found her yet?* Don't do that to yourself. Don't fret about finding your soul mate. And especially after you're married and you're having difficulties, don't tell your pastor, "I'm going to file for divorce; he just wasn't the one." The problem with the myth of "the one" is that it assumes that affection is the glue that holds the marriage together, when really it is your commitment to marriage that safeguards the affection. So ditch the myth and get hitched.

SOME ADVICE TO MEN AND WOMEN

Delayed marriage can lead to a number of problems. For starters, it often lengthens adolescence and the youth culture that goes with it. In his *Short Life of Jonathan Edwards*, George Marsden points out that as far as Edwards was concerned, "the most formidable challenge to church piety was a well-developed youth culture, which intersected with the tavern culture."[2] One of the main reasons for this youth culture, Marsden notes, was the postponing of marriage in Northampton. Because the supply of land had run out in Edwards's town, there were few places for new couples to start their new families. And as result, new families just didn't get started. The average age of marriage had risen to twenty-nine years old for men and twenty-five for women. This meant that young people, instead of getting married, settling down, and having a family, found it difficult to establish themselves independently of their parents and generally made silly and sinful decisions, as twentysomethings tend to do when they have too much time and too little responsibility. That can happen to us too.

> Delayed marriage complicates career decisions, especially for women.

One of the other problems with delayed marriage is that it complicates career decisions, especially for women. There are too many fine Christian women sliding into careers they aren't sure they want to pursue, while they not so secretly wish they could be married and raise a family. I'm not saying women can't work outside the home, let alone that they aren't capable of doing the work quite well. My beef is with the men. While young women are going along with their career path because marriage doesn't seem imminent, young men are meandering through life, putting off marriage, struggling with lust (and sometimes masturbation), and doing nothing much in particular on the job front. When I've spoken on this subject at my church. I've had a number of women tell me afterward, "Preach it, Pastor! We want men to do something. Pursue us. Ask us out. We want to be married, but they need to take some initiative."

Meanwhile, it is all too easy for women to pursue a career and accrue lots of debt while they are single and getting an advanced degree sounds like a good idea. But then they get married at twenty-eight and want to start a family, except now they are in their last year of residency, and they figure they can't quit and "waste" all their training. Plus, they'll need to work at least five years just to pay back school loans. Please do not misunderstand. This is not a criticism of women doctors, nurses, or businesswomen. It's just that their lives are much more complicated because marriage has been delayed. A young woman may feel that she can't get married until she finishes school and pays off her debts.

Sometimes when a couple with debts or young careers get married, their decisions about birth control and family planning —difficult decisions on which Christians can disagree—seem to already have been made for them. This is a tough spot to be in. There are always hard decisions to make and choppy waters to navigate, but I suspect some stories would turn out differently if growing up happened sooner, and men were thinking seriously of marriage at twenty-one instead of thirty-one.

I know I've been pretty hard on my generation, especially the men. I don't write as one who is the model of manly courage or decision making. And I don't write to crush your spirits. Remember, even if we have made mistakes—or are in the middle of mistakes—God loves to help the helpless. He loves to forgive the brokenhearted and give second and third chances to those who've gone through a dozen mistakes already. The Spirit is stronger than our timidity and wiser than our foolishness. But instead of "letting go and letting God," we need to make every effort to grow up in our faith (2 Peter 1:5ff).

WHAT CAN I DO?

As a fellow undershepherd, I encourage all the pastors reading this book to preach to the young people in their congregation to start acting like eighteen is twenty-eight, instead of thinking thirty-eight is eighteen. Do not coddle them (or me!) with low expectations.

Next, I encourage older Christians to set a good example of steady, faithful responsibility; to model Christ-centered consistency and risky decision making for the glory of God; and to be honest with the rest of us about when you have failed and where you are struggling to live up to the good example you want to set.

I encourage the women to consider the long-term ramifications of their decisions when they are twenty-five and single, hoping to be thirty-five and married with children some day.

Finally, I exhort the men reading this book to pray for wisdom (James 1:5–6), get a job, and get married. And do it sooner rather than later. To do so would be good for your sanctification, good for your purity, good for the church, and good for some godly woman out there who would be your wife, though she's probably already better than you deserve, just like my bride was for me.

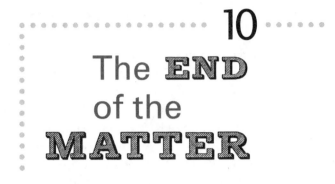

The END
of the
MATTER

I have two living grandparents—both old Dutch men with sharp minds, strong wills, and full heads of white hair. Peter DeYoung is my dad's dad. I've mentioned him a few times already. Menser Vanden Heuvel is my mom's dad. He was born in 1918 in a small farming community outside of Zeeland, Michigan.[1] He was one of nine children and, from what I gather, did not suffer fools gladly. As a young boy, after a friend and he were being picked on, Grandpa Van told his friend, "If they start something tonight, I'm going to knock the tar out of the younger guy and when he's down, you hold him down." When I think of my Grandpa Van now, I think of how proud he is that I'm a pastor and how warmly he smiles at all his grandkids and great-grandkids. But I've known him long enough to imagine that back in the day you probably didn't mess around with Menser.

Grandpa Van didn't go to school past the eighth grade, but

he never stopped learning, and he certainly never stopped working hard. By age twelve, at the beginning of the Great Depression, he was splitting time on the farm and at a machinery shop in town, where he was paid in bundles of green firewood. (Grandpa has always had a knack for mechanics and fixing things, a trait that landed squarely with my cousins more than with me or any of my siblings). At sixteen or seventeen, he and a buddy went to wait in line for work at American Seating Company in Grand Rapids. They waited through the morning and afternoon, only to hear, "Sorry, nothing today." They came back the next day, and the next, and the next. Finally, the foreman said, "If these two want to work that bad, let's put them on." So they got a full-time job building church furniture during the Great Depression for the princely wage of forty cents an hour. "We were rich," Grandpa told me.

Within a few years, Grandpa owned and operated several service stations in town. He was only twenty or twenty-one at the time—the age most "kids" today are still playing video games, sneaking off to parties, and trying to "find" themselves. In talking with my grandpa about his life, I asked whether he wrestled with God's will, or remembered waiting for a sense of direction before taking so much initiative in life as a young man. "No," he said. "I felt like God was waiting for me to get involved." I wonder how many of us are just the opposite—waiting for God to tell us what to do rather than assuming He's waiting for us to go out and be obedient.

Grandpa Van was thinking specifically about Christian Endeavor (CE), the cutting-edge youth program of the day.

Grandpa felt called to work with the young people in CE. The only problem was he belonged to the Christian Reformed Church (CRC), and CE was a program in the local Reformed Church in America (RCA) congregation. Now, to most outsiders, these two denominations seem almost indistinguishable, but if you've ever lived in west Michigan or northwest Iowa or any other Dutch enclave, you would know that the CRC and RCA are siblings separated by a common history. They are kissing cousins who have never kissed and made up. So when my grandpa told his CRC elders that he wanted to work with the RCA-sponsored Christian Endeavor, they let him have it. (I'll take his word for it.) No CRC boy had any business collaborating with the RCA. They pointed fingers, read him the riot act, and did a masterful job of ticking him off.

So Grandpa stood up straight and spoke right to their faces: "And I suppose

> "God's will carried me through . . . and put me in the Air Force."

that you have a special corner in heaven just for the Christian Reformed." And that's how my Grandpa became an RCA man. He's told me the story of getting kicked out of the CRC more than any other story I remember from him. And he always tells it with a bit of a smile. I should add that after more than sixty-five years away, he's now happily rejoined the CRC, going to a fine church that sits just behind his suburban condo.

Grandpa married a wonderful Lutheran woman named

Mildred from northern Michigan in 1941 and got drafted less than a year later. He left for Fort Custer in Battle Creek. There he was examined to see which branch of the armed forces suited him best. He had never even seen the inside of a high school, but "God's will carried me through those exams and put me in the Air Force, which is what I wanted all along." Because he had been in the National Guard for three years, Grandpa was put in charge of the drill at basic training. He eventually wound up in the South Pacific, working on B-29s and taking heavy fire from the Japanese.

When he came back to Michigan and Mildred in 1945, he went to Grand Rapids to be an airplane mechanic. But he needed a civilian license. So he maneuvered his way into college—quite a trick since he had never been to high school—passed some classes, and got his necessary credentials. Several years later, Grandpa started his own airfreight business, which he owned and operated for over twenty years, and made a pretty nice living doing it. Through it all, he raised three kids and stayed very active in the church—teaching high school Sunday school, having the youth over for hayrides, and even working with a Japanese ministry later in life.

GIVING CREDIT WHERE CREDIT IS DUE

At some point in the story, I'm not sure when, he got twenty acres outside of Battle Creek in exchange for a plane he had fixed up. Then he got twenty more acres and another twenty, until he had enough to start farming and get into the cattle business. As he accumulated more land, he would dredge up the swampland and sell the soil. The whole marshy lowland became a man-made lake dug out by my grandpa and his trusty crane.

He always made sure I had some good work to do when I visited during the summer—hauling rocks from the peat, helping to plant a few trees, and standing by scared stiff as my grandpa killed an occasional snapping turtle that threatened his swans. (In my memory I actually participated in the heroic deeds of turtle carnage, but according to my brother and grandpa, my contribution was more akin to tiptoeing away backward and crying like a little girl.)

He lost Grandma to heart trouble in 1990 and remarried a year later.

> "Hard work, sure, but I know it was from God."

Not long ago I asked my grandpa, "Is there anything you think younger generations of Christians have lost that your generation understood?"

"Oh yes," he said quietly.

"Like what, Grandpa?"

He thought for a moment. When he opened his mouth, he didn't answer the question directly, but I got his point, and it was good one. "I started with nothing," he stated. "What right did I have to hope for all these things that fell into place? Hard work, sure, but I know it was from God."

Compared with my affluent, lazy, trivial, tinkering generation, my grandpa would be a remarkable man, except that so many from his generation seem to have been so remarkable. He had his faults, to be sure, but Grandpa Van, like most of the WWII crowd, certainly did something rather than nothing. He worked hard, took chances, showed constant initiative, and, by his own account, lived a pretty fulfilled life—all without searching desperately for fulfillment. He prayed, but didn't hyper-spiritualize his every move. He had several different jobs, but never in hopes of finding the next best thing.

More importantly, growing up in the Depression, he expected little from life, so when he got little he wasn't surprised, and when he got a lot, he chalked it up to God's doing, not his. I sense from talking to my grandpa that he labored hard at everything except trying to discern some mysterious, hidden will of direction from God. Not that he didn't believe in God's providence. Far from it. But the providence he believed in helped him take chances instead of taking breaks. And now that his life is almost done, it helps him trace God's hand of blessing over nine decades gone by and trust the Lord for whatever years lay ahead.

That's Grandpa's life in God. And that's how it should be for the Christian: active in the present, grateful for the past, and hopeful for the future.

A LIFE LIVED NOT IN VAIN

Ecclesiastes may seem a strange book, but it's more relevant than ever. Too many of us are chasing after the wind, looking for satisfaction in work, family, and success—all good things, yet all things that don't ultimately satisfy. It would be bad enough if we were just restless, meandering through life, and a little cowardly. But we've spiritualized restless and meandering cowardice, making it feel like piety instead of passivity. We're not only living lives of vanity; our passion for God is often nothing more than a passion to have God make our search for vanity a successful one.

We need to hear the conclusion of Ecclesiastes: "Fear God and keep his commandments, for this is the whole duty of man" (12:13). If you are going to be anxious about one thing, be anxious to keep His commandments. If we must fear something—and we all do—fear God, not the future.

The will of God isn't a special direction here or a bit of secret knowledge there. God doesn't put us in a maze, turn out the lights, and tell us, "Get out and good luck." In one sense, we trust in the will of God as His sovereign plan for our future. In another sense, we obey the will of God as His good word for our lives. In no sense should we be scrambling around trying to turn to the right page in our personal choose-your-own-adventure novel.

God's will for your life and my life is simpler, harder, and easier than that. Simpler, because there are no secrets we must discover. Harder, because denying ourselves, living for others, and obeying God is more difficult than taking a new job and moving to Fargo. Easier, because as Augustine said, God commands what He wills and grants what He commands.

In other words, God gives His children the will to walk in His ways—not by revealing a series of next steps cloaked in shadows, but by giving us a heart to delight in His law.

So the end of the matter is this: Live for God. Obey the Scriptures. Think of others before yourself. Be holy. Love Jesus. And as you do these things, do whatever else you like, with whomever you like, wherever you like, and you'll be walking in the will of God.

Acknowledgments

When I co-wrote my book *Why We're Not Emergent*, I thanked everyone under the sun. I didn't know if I'd get published again, so I figured I'd better give a shout-out to as many people as possible. This time I'll be briefer, not because there are fewer people to thank, but because I kind of shot my wad the first time around.

The folks at Moody Publishers have once again been a pleasure to work with. Thanks for getting excited about yet another book on the will of God.

Andrew Wolgemuth has been a great help and encouragement to me in this project. His edits and suggestions were invariably helpful. My colleagues in ministry, Doug Phillips and Jason Helopoulos, read through an early draft of the manuscript and offered good encouragement and several helpful suggestions as well.

I've spoken on the will of God a number of times in a

number of different church settings. I'm grateful to the folks from FRCOC, SCF, URC, and the OPC for listening eagerly (or at least faking it), asking probing questions, and engaging me in good conversation about this topic. I wouldn't have thought to write this book except for the encouraging responses I've received in teaching through this material.

If I weren't a Calvinist, I would say I am a very lucky man to be at such a good church. But I know it is only by God's grace and favorable providence that I can serve as pastor at University Reformed Church. To cite just one example, I am thankful for the generous time off I get each year to read and write.

As always, my wife, Trisha, has been my constant support, cheering me on and freeing me up. She is a smiling delight. My children—Ian, Jacob, and Elizabeth—deserve to get their names in another book too.

Finally, I'm thankful for my grandpa DeYoung, along with his new wife, Jo Ann, and my grandpa Vanden Heuvel, along with his wife, Pauline, for agreeing to be interviewed for the book. I gladly dedicate this book to my grandfathers, remembering with gratitude also my deceased grandmothers, June DeYoung and Mildred Vanden Heuvel.

NOTES

CHAPTER 1: THE LONG ROAD TO NOWHERE

1. Robert Wuthnow. *After the Baby Boomers: How Twenty- and Thirty-Somethings Are Shaping the Future of American Religion* (Princeton, N.J.: Princeton Univ. Press, 2007).

2. Ibid., 11.

3. Christian Smith, "Get a Life: The Challenge of Emerging Adulthood," *Books & Culture*, November/December 2007, 10.

CHAPTER 2: THE WILL OF GOD IN CHRISTIANESE

1. *Ecumenical Creeds and Reformed Confessions* (Grand Rapids: Faith Alive Christian Resources, 1988), Question and Answer 27.

2. Gerald Sittser, *The Will of God as a Way of Life: Finding and Following the Will of God* (Grand Rapids: Zondervan, 2000), 17.

CHAPTER 3: DIRECTIONALLY CHALLENGED

1. I'm grateful to Doug Phillips, a Baptist pastor in Lansing, Michigan, and friend of mine, for bringing this verse and its application to my attention.

2. Bruce Waltke, *Finding the Will of God: A Pagan Notion?* (Grand Rapids: Eerdmans, 1995), 15.

3. Barry Schwartz, *The Paradox of Choice: Why More is Less* (New York: HarperCollins, 2005), 9–10.

4. Ibid., 141.

CHAPTER 4: OUR MAGIC 8-BALL GOD

1. The first three problems are also covered by Gerald Sittser, *The Will of God as a Way of Life* (Grand Rapids: Zondervan, 2000), 18–24. Obviously, I have borrowed from his wisdom, and not the other way around.

2. In case you're unfamiliar with the expression, college girls sometimes talk about "dating" Jesus as the reason why they can't give the time of day to would-be suitors.

3. As quoted in Mark Chanski, *Manly Dominion* (Merrick, N.Y.: Calvary Press, 2004), 84.

4. John Eldredge, *Walking With God: Talk to Him. Hear From Him. Really.* (Nashville: Nelson, 2008).

5. This is not everything that needs to be said about the law and the Christian. We are in one sense not under law and in another sense still expected to obey its principles.

CHAPTER 5: A BETTER WAY?

1. See John Piper, *The Purifying Power of Living by Faith in Future Grace* (Sisters, Oreg.: Multnomah, 1998), 51–64.

2. Gerald Sittser, *The Will of God as a Way of Life* (Grand Rapids: Zondervan, 2000), 28.

CHAPTER 6: ORDINARY GUIDANCE AND SUPERNATURAL SURPRISES

1. My five statements are derived from, and in some places identical to the statements offered by Phillip D. Jensen and Tony Payne, *Guidance and the Voice of God* (Kingsford, NSW [Australia: Matthias], 1997), 63–81.

2. Bruce Waltke, *Finding the Will of God: A Pagan Notion?* (Grand Rapids: Eerdmans, 2002), 18–19. Tim Challies makes the same point in his fine book, *The Discipline of Spiritual Discernment* (Wheaton, Ill.: Crossway, 2007): "When we have ruled out what God has expressly forbidden, and when we have searched the Bible and prayed for wisdom, we are free to choose. This seems to be what is modeled for us in the New Testament. We do not find people desperately seeking God's will through dreams or visions (though occasionally God saw fit to use such miraculous means), but we see people making decisions based on what seemed good or best or necessary" (116).

3. Ibid., 19.

4. Vern Sheridan Poythress, "Modern Spiritual Gifts as Analogous to Apostolic Gifts: Affirming Extraordinary Works of the Spirit Within Cessationist Theology," *Journal of the Evangelical Theological Society* 39, no. 1 (1996): 101.

5. Quoted in Wayne Grudem, *Systematic Theology* (Grand Rapids: Zondervan, 1995), 1041.

CHAPTER 7: TOOLS OF THE TRADE

1. The faux-story posted at www.larknews.com can be found in print in Joel Kilpatrick, *A Field Guide to Evangelicals and Their Habitat* (San Francisco: HarperOne, 2006), 16.

2. Thanks to my friend Jason Helopoulos, a fine young Presbyterian Church of America pastor in my area, for pointing out this illustration from the book of Jonah.

3. See Judges 6:36–40.

4. As quoted in Mark Chanski, *Manly Dominion* (Merrick, N.Y.: Calvary Press, 2004), 111.

5. "John Newton on Divine Guidance" in *Guard Us, Guide Us: Divine Leading in Life's Decisions* by J. I. Packer and Carolyn Nystrom (Grand Rapids: Baker, 2008), 244.

6. Ibid., 246.

CHAPTER 8: THE WAY OF WISDOM

1. Along these lines, I highly recommend the book by C. John Sommerville, *How the News Makes Us Dumb: The Death of Wisdom in an Information Society* (Downers Grove, Ill.: InterVarsity, 1999).

CHAPTER 9: WORK, WEDLOCK, AND GOD'S WILL

1. Robert Wuthnow, *After the Baby Boomers* (Princeton, N.J.: Princeton Univ. Press, 2007), 22.

2. George Marsden, *A Short Life of Jonathan Edwards* (Grand Rapids: Eerdmans, 2008), 44.

CHAPTER 10: THE END OF THE MATTER

1. Special thanks to my grandpa for allowing me to interview him and learn more of his story. I'm very grateful too for the fine piece of oral history, "The Life of Menser Vanden Heuvel," which has been transcribed and bound by my aunt, Carol Vanden Heuvel Shaw.